With the inspiration of (and apologies to) Northern Pacific's grand old slogan,
"Main Street of the Northwest."
NP caboose on display at the Kingdome in Seattle, 1985.

Deep in the Blue Mountains of Oregon, a UP *Old Timers Special* meets an eastbound freight—both on the roll—at Hilgard, April 20, 1979.

MAIN STREETS
of the
NORTHWEST

Rails from the Rockies to the Pacific

Volume 1 Oregon • Idaho • Montana
T.O. Repp

TRANS-ANGLO BOOKS
GLENDALE, CALIFORNIA

MAIN STREETS OF THE NORTHWEST

Printed and bound in the United States of America

Published by TRANS-ANGLO BOOKS, a division of INTERURBAN PRESS
P.O. Box 6444 • Glendale, California 91225

FIRST PRINTING: FALL 1989

Library of Congress Cataloging-in-Publication Data

Repp, T. O.
    Main streets of the Northwest : rails from the Rockies to the Pacific / T. O. Repp.
      p.   cm.
    Bibliography: p.
    Includes index.
    ISBN 0-87046-085-4 (v. 1)
    1. Railroads—Northwest, Pacific.   I. Title.
TF23.7.R46   1989
385′.09795—dc20   89-15467
                                                CIP

Acknowledgements

THE AUTHOR WISHES to express his appreciation to the following people and organizations for their support in the preparation of this work.

Jim Mattson, Art Jacobsen, Bob Melbo and Walt Grande for checking the historic data; Jim and Barb Berg and Ed Sherry for reviewing the manuscript, layouts and captions; and special thanks to the Seattle Museum of History and Industry, whose collection of timetables and BN-donated historic material proved to be invaluable.

Thanks must be also given to George Krause, SP public relations, and Howard Kallio, BN public relations. Various offices and agencies of the Burlington Northern, Camas Prairie, Nezperce, Oregon Pacific and Eastern, Oregon and Northwestern, Rarus, Southern Pacific, St. Maries River, Union Pacific and Weyerhaeuser Woods railroads also provided welcome assistance.

Finally, thanks are extended to the countless depot operators and train crews encountered along the way for their willingness to share information, and their enthusiasm and friendliness.

(Back cover) Mount Hood dwarfs its namesake railroad as a three-car train backs up Hood River Canyon on August 27, 1982.

(Front cover left) BN, Frisco and Western Pacific geeps take train No. 170 across Crooked River Gorge on September 11, 1979. The bridge was the country's second highest when completed in 1911, SP's original Pecos River bridge, at 321 feet, was 12 inches higher.

(Front cover right) An SP&S RS-3 shares space with an NP RS-11 at the Hoyt Street Roundhouse March 22, 1975.

Duotones and Image Assembly: Jim Walter Color Separation, Beloit, WI
Design and Production: William L. Bradley & James W. Reese
Typography: Roc-Pacific, Los Angeles, CA
Printing and Bindery: Walsworth Publishing, Marceline, MO

Contents

Introduction

NORTHERN PACIFIC introduced its "Main Street of the Northwest" slogan on locomotives, freight cars and cabooses in the 1940s to promote a new, postwar image. It seemed appropriate, for it would be hard to imagine the Northwest without railroads, NP or otherwise.

Main Streets of the Northwest is dedicated to that sentiment, documenting the spectacle of Northwest railroading from 1969 to 1988. Because of the size and scope of the work, two volumes have been prepared: Oregon–Idaho Panhandle–Western Montana and Washington–Western Canada.

Volume One begins with Oregon, where Northwest railroading began. Next is the Idaho Panhandle, where an amazing variety of railroading has been packed into an area barely 50 miles wide. Finally, there is Western Montana, under whose Big Skies three transcontinental railroads were built, more than in any Rocky Mountain state.

Volume Two looks at Washington and Western Canadian railroading, from SP&S's "North Bank Road" along the Columbia River to BC Rail's high-tech Tumbler Subdivision, and from Simpson Timber Company log trains on the Olympic Peninsula to Canadian Pacific's spiral tunnels in the Rockies.

Chapters are arranged by region, railroad or operational hub (e.g., Klamath Falls, Sandpoint, Spokane), so the division between chapters and/or volumes may appear somewhat arbitrary, especially along the Washington–Idaho border. Both volumes do include all contemporary main lines, short lines and a majority of branch lines (though for practical reasons, some of the smaller operations have been omitted).

Main Streets spans a particularly turbulent period of Northwest railroading. The 1970 Burlington Northern merger robbed much of the region's individuality as did the 1971 inauguration of Amtrak, which resulted in the passing of such institutions as UP's *Butte Special* and Oregon Trunk's mixed train to Bend. Together these events represented the most significant change in Northwest railroading since the coming of diesels and streamlined trains.

More recently, the Northwest has suffered the loss of the Milwaukee Road, BN's Wallace Branch and the Oregon and Northwestern, to name a few. Marginal operations being closely watched include Southern Pacific's Tillamook Branch, Camas Prairie's Grangeville Branch, and Canadian Pacific's Princeton Subdivision, all of which are included in these volumes.

Beyond the transition to Cascade Green and Platinum Mist, *Main Streets* takes a look at the renaissance of steam locomotives as well as the survival of first-generation diesels. There are visits to railroad yards, roundhouses and stations. And throughout these pages, there is always an intentional sense of place: from the canyons of the Deschutes and Fraser to mountain passes named Kicking Horse and Stampede, and from busy rail centers in Portland and Spokane to quiet little places like Avery, Lester and Lombard.

Interesting times, interesting places. For this writer, who began his Northwest journey with a trip aboard the *North Coast Limited* in 1950 (at the impressionable age of three), it's been quite an adventure.

Northwest Passages

EVERY RAILROAD in the Northwest today has a story to tell, for each played a key role in the development of this vast region. Towns like Pasco, Everett and Great Falls owe their very existence to the railroads; so does much of the region's history.

Northwest railroads got their start along the Columbia River in the 1850s, where mule-driven trains riding on wooden rails began moving freight around unnavigable portions of the river. The promise of federal land grants helped build the Northern Pacific Railway and the Oregon and California Railroad, while north of the 49th parallel, British Columbia considered the completion of the Canadian Pacific transcontinental a condition of its inclusion in the Canadian Confederation. But beyond bringing supplies into the Northwest, there were enormous resources of minerals, timber and agriculture to ship out.

Coal deposits on Vancouver Island led to the construction of numerous colliery railways and in 1863, western Canada's first steam locomotive, the British-built *Pioneer,* arrived to work the docks in Nanaimo. Rich ore deposits in southern British Columbia, Idaho's Coeur d'Alene Mountains and Butte lured branch lines into the hills, some of which still carry ore to this day.

Northwest timber soon found a market in the growing cities and towns, assisted by a network of logging railroads that was almost as dense as the forests. One such enterprise on Vancouver Island dispensed with rails altogether, preferring to run its double-flanged wheel Climax locomotive on logs. With the advent of logging trucks and better highways, however, most logging railroads have long since vanished; those that remain have reached near-legendary status in the eyes of railfans.

A growing demand for wheat in the late 19th century resulted in more long-term problems than short-term profits for some railroads. In the Palouse region of Eastern Washington, for example, both the Northern Pacific and the Oregon Railway and Navigation Company built an extensive network of granger lines that rivaled anything in the Midwest. Though some of these branch lines still exist, trucks and river barges have rendered most of them surplus and unprofitable. The problem was much worse in Canada because of the 1897 Crows Nest Pass Rate, wherein the Canadian Pacific Railway agreed to receive a construction subsidy for its Crows Nest Pass line in exchange for a promise to haul grain anywhere for 0.5 cents per ton-mile—forever. Over the years "The Crow" has cost the Canadian Pacific millions of dollars in lost revenues. The Canadian government finally rescinded the agreement in 1983, allowing CPR to build a sorely needed new right-of-way across Rogers Pass.

If towering mountains and deep canyons weren't enough to discourage railroad building, the economic depressions (known then as "Panics") of 1873 and 1893 certainly did. Ben Holladay lost control of his Oregon and California Railroad during the "Panic of 1873" as did Northern Pacific's major investor, Jay Cooke & Company (which, ironically, started the Panic). As a result, the O&C, NP and countless other railroads were forced to suspend construction for many years.

The worst financial crisis of the era occurred in 1893, when 193 U.S. railroads declared bankruptcy, including all Northwest lines except James J. Hill's Great Northern Railway. Hill took advantage of depressed stock prices and acquired control of the Northern Pacific, Burlington and several smaller lines. Financier Edward H. Harriman acquired the Union Pacific in 1897 and the Southern Pacific in 1901 in much the same manner. By the turn of the century, Hill and Harriman controlled every major railroad in the American Northwest.

But neither Hill nor Harriman could compare with Henry Villard's earlier command of Northwest transportation. Born in Bavaria, Villard emigrated to America in 1853 and became a journalist, covering the Lincoln-Douglas debates and the Civil War. In 1874 he was asked by a group of German investors to salvage Ben Holladay's floundering Oregon and California Railroad. Villard soon began acquiring other properties for himself, including the Oregon Railway and Navigation Company, the Northern Pacific Railway, the *New York Evening Post,* and had enough money left over to help Thomas Edison start the Edison (General) Electric Company.

Not all Northwest railroaders were entrepreneurs; J.J. Hill's longtime associate and chief engineer, John F. Stevens, was a notable example. Stevens located the Great Northern main line over Marias Pass in Montana and continued the GN route west to a Cascade mountain pass that now bears his name. After a brief term as vice president of the New Haven Railroad, he became president of the Spokane Portland and Seattle and built the Oregon Trunk Railway. Perhaps Stevens' greatest achievement was his assignment as Chief Engineer on the Panama Canal, though his subsequent five-year assignment on the Trans-Siberian Railway should not be overlooked either.

And that's how Northwest railroads were built—with the help of bountiful resources, beset at times by an unpredictable economy, but always with a sense of vision and promise.

Oregon

FROM ITS EARLY beginnings along the Columbia River to present-day operations throughout the state, Oregon railroading has always been characterized by a combination of pioneer spirit and Yankee ingenuity. Soon after New Englanders began arriving in the 1840s by way of the Oregon Trail, Oregon became the Northwest's first state (and only state for 30 years). It also became home to the Northwest's first standard-gauge railroad, first steam and diesel locomotives, and first streamliner.

Oregon's first railroad was a simple portage line built along the Columbia River in the 1850s. Twenty years later, Ben Holladay was busy pushing his Oregon and California Railroad toward the California border. Northern Pacific brought the first transcontinental trains from the Midwest in 1883 (via Oregon Railway and Navigation's Columbia River line) and the following year, the OR&N met Union Pacific's Oregon Short Line on the far side of the Blue Mountains, creating a second Northwest transcontinental route. A connection to California was completed via Siskiyou Summit in 1887, supplemented in 1926 by one of the most ambitious mainline bypasses in history, Southern Pacific's 275-mile Natron Cutoff via Klamath Falls.

As the twentieth century began, Edward H. Harriman and James J. Hill, two of the most influential railroad men of their time, began to make their presence known in Oregon. Harriman was in control of the UP, SP and OR&N, while Hill had the GN and NP (and later, the Spokane Portland and Seattle, Oregon Electric and Oregon Trunk). The two locked horns on several occasions, but never so dramatically as in the Deschutes River Canyon where the last great railroad war of the Old West took place.

But one should not overlook such lesser figures as Colonel T. Egenton Hogg, whose Oregon Pacific might have extended across the state from Yaquina Bay to the Idaho border, or Robert Strahorn, whose Oregon California and Eastern might have connected Klamath Falls with Burns, Bend and Lakeview. Such grand ambitions were never to be realized, though much of their completed trackage survives today.

There is ample evidence to suggest that Oregonians have always been ardent railroad boosters. Faced with the prospect of being bypassed by the Oregon Trunk, the townsfolk of Prineville built and financed their own line using secondhand rail and volunteer labor. Certainly Portland's loan of steam engine SP4449 to the American Freedom Train Foundation in 1975 cannot be overlooked, but perhaps no better example of dedication can be offered than patrons of the resurrected Sumpter Valley Railway who have recreated a part of this narrow-gauge legend with their bare hands.

Images of Oregon railroading today include long strings of lumber-laden flatcars threading through rainy coastal forests, fast container trains hurrying along the Columbia Gorge, and Amtrak Superliners arriving at Portland's Union Station—images as strong and diverse as the geography, history and people that created them.

Much has been accomplished here since the early days. Messrs. Harriman and Hill would no doubt be impressed.

An Oregon and Northwestern freight from Seneca passes through Trout Creek Canyon near Silvies on August 23, 1982.

Southern Pacific's Tillamook Hauler crosses the west fork of Dairy Creek near Buxton on July 12, 1980. Classic Oregon railroading this: lush forests, timber trestles, ageless SD9s.

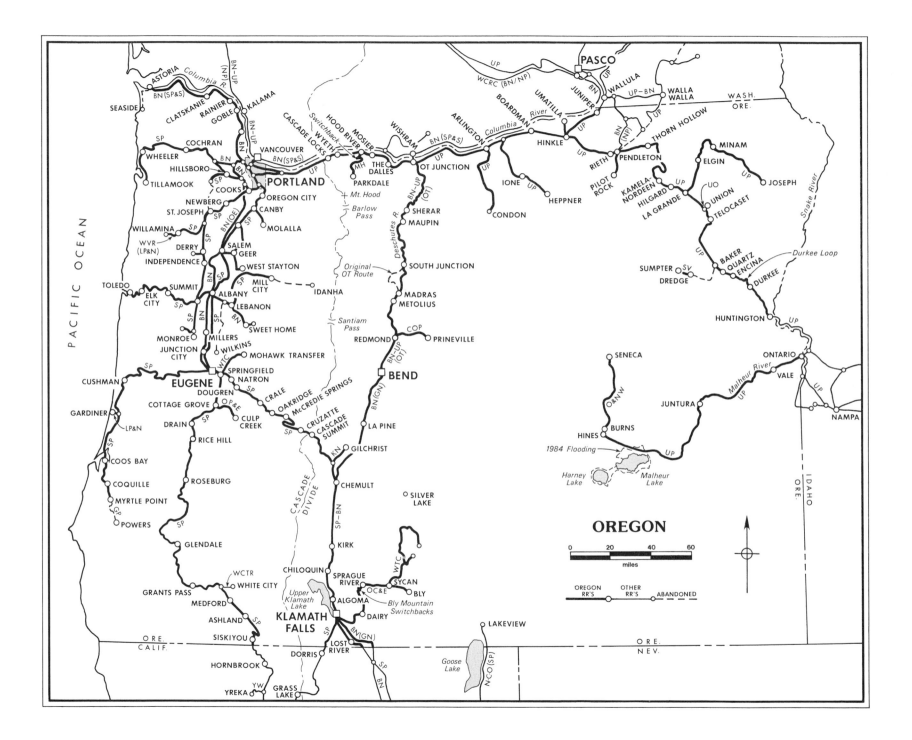

PACIFIC OCEAN

SEASIDE

ASTORIA
Columbia
CLATSKANIE
BN (SP&S)
RAINIER
GOBLE
KALAMA
BN-UP
(NP)R.

COCHRAN
WHEELER
HILLSBORO
TILLAMOOK
COOKS
NEWBERG
ST. JOSEPH
WILLAMINA
WVR (LP&N)
DERRY
INDEPENDENCE
TOLEDO
ELK CITY
SUMMIT
ALBANY
MONROE
MILLERS
JUNCTION CITY
WILKINS
WTC
MOHAWK TRANSFER

VANCOUVER
BN (SP&S)
PORTLAND
OREGON CITY
CANBY
MOLALLA
SALEM
GEER
WEST STAYTON
MILL CITY
LEBANON
SWEET HOME

CUSHMAN
GARDINER
LP&N
COTTAGE GROVE
DRAIN
RICE HILL
COOS BAY
COQUILLE
MYRTLE POINT
GP
POWERS

EUGENE
SPRINGFIELD
NATRON
DOUGREN
CRALE
OP&E
CULP CREEK
OAKRIDGE
McCREDIE SPRINGS
CRUZATTE
CASCADE SUMMIT
ROSEBURG
GLENDALE

CASCADE DIVIDE

GRANTS PASS
WCTR
WHITE CITY
MEDFORD
ASHLAND
SISKIYOU
HORNBROOK
YW
YREKA
GRASS LAKE
DORRIS

CASCADE LOCKS
Switchback
WYETH
HOOD RIVER
MOSIER
MH
THE DALLES
PARKDALE
Mt. Hood
Barlow Pass
Original OT Route
Deschutes R.
BN-UP (OT)
SHERAR
MAUPIN
SOUTH JUNCTION
Santiam Pass
MADRAS
METOLIUS
REDMOND
COP
PRINEVILLE
IDANHA

BEND
BN(GN)
LA PINE
KN
GILCHRIST
CHEMULT
SP-BN
KIRK
CHILOQUIN
SPRAGUE RIVER
WTC
SYCAN
OC&E
BLY
Bly Mountain Switchbacks
ALGOMA
DAIRY
Upper Klamath Lake
KLAMATH FALLS
SP
LOST RIVER
BN(GN)
SP

SILVER LAKE

WISHRAM
BN (SP&S)
ARLINGTON
Columbia
BOARDMAN
UMATILLA
River
OT JUNCTION
HINKLE
UP
IONE
UP
HEPPNER
CONDON
RIETH
PENDLETON
PILOT ROCK
BN (NP)
THORN HOLLOW

PASCO
WCRC (BN/NP)
JUNIPER
BN
WALLULA
UP-BN
WALLA WALLA
WASH. ORE.

MINAM
ELGIN
KAMELA-NORDEEN
HILGARD
LA GRANDE
UO
UNION
TELOCASET
JOSEPH
UP

SUMPTER
DREDGE
SV
BAKER
QUARTZ
ENCINA
DURKEE
Durkee Loop
HUNTINGTON
UP

SENECA
O&NW
BURNS
HINES
1984 Flooding
Harney Lake
Malheur Lake
JUNTURA
Malheur River
UP

ONTARIO
VALE
UP
NAMPA
IDAHO ORE.

LAKEVIEW
Goose Lake
NCO (SP)
ORE. NEV.

OREGON

| 0 | 20 | 40 | 60 |

miles

OREGON RR'S   OTHER RR'S   ABANDONED

Oregon railroading, clockwise from above: Oregon, California and Eastern yards at Sycan, June 19, 1984; SP4449 with Amtrak's *Transcontinental Steam Excursion* at Cascade Summit, April 30, 1977; a 50-car Oregon Electric freight near Harrisburg, August 8, 1987; Amtrak's *Pioneer* and a Union Pacific/Norfolk and Western freight at Nolin, near Pendleton, September 15, 1979.

Rails Along the Columbia

IT IS APPROPRIATE to begin with the railroads of the Columbia River, for this mightiest of all Northwest tributaries provides the only water-level passage through the Cascade Mountains north of California and south of British Columbia. It's also where mule-driven wagons riding on wooden rails had the distinction (in 1851) of being the first railroad to operate on the West Coast.

This pioneering conveyance was built along the north bank of the river to provide a detour around Cascade Rapids. A decade later, the five-foot-gauge Oregon Portage Railroad was completed on the opposite shore where the *Oregon Pony,* the Northwest's first steam locomotive, made its debut in 1862.

The Oregon Steam Navigation Company took control of all river traffic east of Portland in 1862, purchasing the Oregon Portage Railroad and building another (around Celilo Falls east of The Dalles) in the process. In 1879, Henry Villard merged OSN and Oregon Steamship Company holdings to form the Oregon Railway and Navigation Company. One of OR&N's first priorities was to extend the narrow-gauge rails of its subsidiary Walla Walla and Columbia River Railroad from Wallula to The Dalles, not simply to supplement water transportation, but to keep the Northern Pacific from acquiring the route.

By the time OR&N's narrow-gauge rails reached Coyote (near Boardman) in 1881, it had been decided to convert them to standard gauge. The portage railroad located at The Dalles was standard gauged in February 1880 and extended eastward, reaching Coyote on April 4, 1881. (The Wallula–Coyote segment was standard gauged two weeks later.)

The OR&N next directed its efforts west of The Dalles, where railroad building proved to be more difficult. More than eight miles of trestlework had to be built, and cuts and tunnels had to be blasted through solid rock. Rails from Portland and The Dalles were joined on October 4, 1882, at Bonneville (near Cascade Locks), where a silver spike ceremony marked the completion of an all-rail route between Portland and Wallula (and Spokane via the NP).

NP trains began operating over the OR&N into Portland in 1883. Union Pacific's entry into the region via the Blue Mountains and the completion of NP's route across the Cascades led to the lease of OR&N's Columbia River line to the UP in 1887.

In more recent times, the entire right-of-way between Bonneville and Hinkle has been relocated and straightened due to the construction of several dams and the Columbia River Highway. The improvement in running times has been dramatic, especially east of The Dalles where trains routinely cruise at 80 mph.

Even with most of the original OR&N line now obliterated or submerged, the endless passage of trains along the Columbia each day is clear evidence that Henry Villard's handiwork is still very much intact.

On June 23, 1978, GP30 No. 859 pulls eastbound tonnage past a local at Cascade Locks, where Columbia River railroading began in 1851.

(Above): The *Oregon Pony*—in remarkably good condition for her age—on display at Cascade Locks. (Right): UP GP7 No. 103 takes a Mount Hood Railroad freight through Pine Grove on August 27, 1982. That's Washington State's Mount Adams (not Mount Hood) in the background.

(Above right): A BN freight prepares to leave the former SP&S depot at Astoria on May 14, 1982. Astoria marks the end of nearly a thousand miles of Northwest rails which follow the course of the Columbia River between the Canadian Rockies and the Pacific.

(Opposite): A U30C–SD24B–GP30B lashup pulls a string of bauxite hoppers across the long fill at Wyeth on April 10, 1977. This and several other long fills replaced miles of twisting right-of-way (some of which is still visible to the left of the train) when the Interstate 80N was completed in the 1960s.

(Left): The 1977 introduction of Amtrak's Seattle–Salt Lake City *Pioneer* marked the return of Columbia Gorge passenger service after an absence of six years. A four-month-old Number 26 is seen here departing Hood River on a rainy October 30, 1977. (Above): UP's OMN (Overland Mail Northwest), once the fastest train between Omaha and the Northwest, rolls westward between Meno and Wyeth on September 16, 1979.

Flagships of the UP Fleet

UP's *Portland Rose* and *City of Portland* were once familiar sights along the Columbia, but with the coming of Amtrak, the only yellow and gray streamliners to be found were company-sponsored passenger specials. Since these scenes were recorded in 1978 and 1979, all but one of UP's E units and a large portion of its passenger car fleet has been sold or scrapped.

(Above): In a rare Northwest appearance, 4-8-4 No. 8444 storms through Boardman with a seven-car Oregon Historical Society Special, bound for La Grande on September 14, 1979. (Right): A quartet of E9s leans into the curves west of The Dalles with the Hinkle Yard Dedication Special, returning to Portland on June 23, 1978.

Hinkle

Located 185 miles east of Portland, Hinkle is home to the largest railroad yard in the Northwest. It was extensively rebuilt in 1978 at a cost of over $20 million, and forms a hub for all UP operations to Portland, Seattle, Spokane, Yakima and points east.

(Above right): SD24 yard goats on the hump at Hinkle, September 15, 1979. SD40s (right) do the chores today.

Mount Hood Railroad

The Mount Hood Railroad was built in 1906–1910 by David and William Eccles of Sumpter Valley Railway fame. The line climbs nearly 1,700 feet from the Columbia River to Parkdale on three-percent grades and a single switchback, which forces trains to operate backward in and out of Hood River. The 22-mile line was acquired by the Union Pacific in October 1968, and sold to Northern Rail Services in 1987.

(Left): Mount Hood dwarfs its namesake railroad as a three-car train backs up Hood River Canyon on August 27, 1982. (Below): Later the same day, the turnout at Switchback has been aligned and the rear brakeman has assumed his position on the caboose as forward observer for the 2½-mile descent into Hood River.

SWITCHBACK

Rails to the Pacific

BN's 95-mile Seaside Branch west of Portland was built as two separate railroads. Northern Pacific built the Portland–Goble segment in 1883–1890 as part of its transcontinental mainline to Tacoma (trains were ferried across the Columbia until the NP–SP&S Columbia River bridge at Portland was opened in 1908). Tracks west of Goble to Astoria and Seaside were built as the Astoria and Columbia River Railroad, completed in 1898. J.J. Hill purchased the A&CR in 1907, transferring its ownership to the SP&S in 1911. The long bridge across Youngs Bay west of Astoria has since been removed, making Astoria the end of the line today.

(Above right): BN's tri-weekly Clatskanie Local (the eastern half of a two-train relay that operates between Astoria and Portland) rumbles down the main street of Rainier on June 3, 1984. (Right): In a late afternoon scene reminiscent of moonlight, the Astoria Local (the western half of the relay) passes a Columbia River freighter just east of Astoria on May 14, 1982.

Portland

A string of "MAX" (Metropolitan Area Express) cars rolls through downtown Portland on October 3, 1987. Within a year of its 1986 debut, MAX ridership exceeded initial estimates by more than 200 percent.

"GRAVITY BUILT THIS TOWN," noted James J. Hill on the occasion of Portland's Lewis and Clark Centennial Exposition in 1905. Located near the confluence of the Willamette and Columbia rivers in the 1840s, Portland soon became an important crossroads for both land and water transportation and along the way, Oregon's largest city.

Today the "Rose City" is the northern terminus of the Espee Empire and the westernmost point of continuous Union Pacific trackage. It is home to major railroad yards for the UP (Albina), SP (Brooklyn), BN (Willbridge) and Portland Terminal (Lake) as well as Union Station, the oldest major railroad station in the west.

Portland's first railroad was the Oregon Central, which began construction toward California in 1868. The Oregon Railway and Navigation's Columbia River line was completed in 1882, allowing transcontinental Northern Pacific trains to reach Portland the following year.

Between 1873 and 1883, Portland passengers and freight bound for Tacoma had to travel by Columbia River steamboat to Kalama (Washington), southern terminus of NP's isolated Tacoma main line. The car ferry *Tacoma* began service in 1883 and the following year, after NP completed a rail line from Portland west to Hunters (across the river from Kalama), a second ferry, the *Kalama*, was added. The Oregon-side ferry slip was moved two miles west to Goble in 1890, but an all-rail route to Tacoma was not achieved until jointly owned SP&S–NP bridges across the Willamette and Columbia rivers in Portland were completed in 1908.

Portland's population approached 200,000 by the turn of the century, and an extensive network of electric interurban lines soon followed: Portland Traction to the southeast, United Railways to the west, and the Oregon Electric and SP's "Red Electrics" to the south. Automobiles forced the abandonment of most interurban service by the early 1930s (the sole exception being Portland Traction, which continued to carry passengers until 1958).

Portland became the first city on the West Coast to welcome a streamliner with the arrival of UP's *City of Portland* in 1935. By 1950, UP had its General Motors *Train of Tomorrow* in Portland–Seattle pool service, while the friendly Southern Pacific was busy running streamlined *Cascades* and *Shasta Daylights* south to California.

Though the interurbans (and the streamliners) are long gone, there's still much to see in Portland: UP freights climbing Sullivan's Gulch, switch engines clanking along the Willamette River waterfront and at night, Union Station's "Go By Train" sign flashing to remind us of the magic of riding trains.

(Above): As this baggage car suggests, Portland was indeed SP&S's middle name. Note the billboard in the background. (Right): A UP grain train skirts the Willamette River en route to Albina Yard on October 4, 1987. The bridge in the background is Portland's "Steel Bridge," which carries highway traffic and MAX light rail on the upper level and UP-SP–Amtrak trains on the lower level.

BEFORE BN:
September 28, 1969

1969 was the last full year of GN, SP&S and NP operations which, along with the UP and SP, brought the total number of Class I railroads operating within the Portland city limits to five. The three Northwest BN predecessors became one in 1970, but a condition of the merger provided the Milwaukee Road access into town (via the BN from Longview, Washington) the same year.

(Above left): Venerable SP&S Alco RS-3s roar through Willbridge with tonnage bound for St. Helens and Astoria. (Left): A GN caboose hop precedes an NP freight at Portland Terminal's busy Lake Yard.

A quartet of NP F7s takes a string of high cars past the Union Station trainsheds (and UP's *City of Portland)* en route to SP's Brooklyn Yard.

UNION STATION

Portland Union Station, built by the NP–UP–SP-owned Northern Pacific Terminal Company in the 1890s, still serves Amtrak passengers today. During its peak years in the 1920s, 90 regular trains and electric inter- urbans arrived and departed here daily.

(Right): By 1969, SP&S's train No. 4 to Spokane (seen here alongside UP's *Portland Rose* on September 27th) had been reduced to little more than a few mail storage cars and a rider coach.

(Left): GN's "Pool Train" No. 459 awaits its 1:30 p.m. departure to Seattle on September 28, 1969 (SP's *Cascade* from Oakland is on the adjacent track). GN, NP and UP Portland–Seattle passenger trains operated in a "pool" (hence the nickname), employ- ing common ticketing and marketing for each of the three trains in service.

TO MAIN CONCOURSE AND TRAINS

	ARRIVALS			DEPARTURES	
27	EMPIRE BUILDER CHICAGO ST PAUL SPOKANE	835 AM	796	MT RAINIER TACOMA SEATTLE	800 AM
26	PIONEER SEATTLE TACOMA	1150 AM	26	PIONEER BOISE OGDEN CHICAGO	1200 N
14	COAST STARLIGHT LOS ANGELES OAKLAND EUGENE	215 PM	14	COAST STARLIGHT TACOMA SEATTLE	230 PM
11	COAST STARLIGHT SEATTLE TACOMA	300 PM	11	COAST STARLIGHT EUGENE OAKLAND LOS ANGELES	315 PM
25	PIONEER CHICAGO OGDEN BOISE	530 PM	28	EMPIRE BUILDER SPOKANE ST PAUL CHICAGO	415 PM
797	MT RAINIER SEATTLE TACOMA	920 PM	25	PIONEER TACOMA SEATTLE	540 PM

(Above): Nearly a century of technology separates Union Station's clock tower from an Amtrak Superliner coach in this 1981 scene. The neon "Union Station/Go By Train" signs (installed in 1948) have since been refurbished, thanks to railfan donations. (Above right): Arrivals and departures at Union Station, July 4, 1982. (Right): Flanges squealing, domes on the 1981 Sacramento Railfair Excursion negotiate the 17-degree curve on Portland's Steel Bridge near Union Station. This was to be the last revenue run for Amtrak domes on the West Coast; shortly thereafter, the cars were shipped to the Midwest.

Willamette Valley Railroads

SD9Es with northbound tonnage at Oregon City, May 1, 1977.

IF REDUCED TO simple geographic averages, Oregon could be characterized as an arid, sparsely populated region situated at an elevation of 3,300 feet. Southern Pacific, with 45 percent of all trackage in the state, would therefore be Oregon's "average" railroad. Most of Oregon, however, lives within the confines of the Willamette Valley, and SP's domination of Oregon railroading there is even more pronounced.

SP's 650-odd miles of Willamette Valley trackage (including its three coast branches) qualify as the most concentrated network of rail anywhere in the Northwest. Only a lone short line, Amtrak and BN's Oregon Electric break SP's monopoly here today. Yet within this network lie the legacies of a narrow-gauge system, two competing north-south land grant railroads and a would-be transcontinental. Most were acquired (rather than built) by the SP and as such, each has its own history.

Willamette Valley's first railroad was the Oregon Central, incorporated by Joseph Gaston after the U.S. Congress passed an Oregon–California railroad land grant bill in 1866. After the OC announced it would build along the west side of the Willamette River, opponents incorporated the Oregon Central *Rail Road* in 1867 to build along the east side. Both celebrated ground-breaking ceremonies in Portland the following April, but neither had the financial resources to do much else.

Ben Holladay, owner of a profitable steamship business along the Pacific Coast, broke the stalemate by acquiring the eastside Oregon Central in October 1868. He then descended upon the Oregon Legislature, which rescinded an earlier pledge to give the land grant to Gaston's westside line. Holladay was the first to complete the 20 miles of track required by Congress (in December 1869) and his Oregon Central was duly awarded the land grant.

With funds obtained from German investors, Holladay's railroad, renamed the Oregon and California Railroad, proceeded southward, reaching Eugene in October 1871 and Roseburg a year later. The Panic of 1873 halted Holladay's plans and Henry Villard, acting as an agent for O&C's German investors, purchased the property in 1876 (and later, virtually every other railroad in the Willamette Valley). Villard's empire collapsed under the strain of completing his Northern Pacific transcontinental and in 1887, the Oregon and California Railroad was leased to the Central Pacific. The entire network of CP-controlled lines and subsidiaries in Oregon was merged into the Southern Pacific on July 1, 1915.

SP retains its virtual monopoly in Willamette Valley railroading today, though few of its operations are profitable. Increasing competition from trucks has caused some branchline trackage to be abandoned, leased or sold, and it is likely that others will suffer the same fate.

The Seattle–Los Angeles *Coast Starlight,* one of Amtrak's most popular trains in the
west, skirts the scenic Willamette River south of Oregon City on October 3, 1987.

SP's VALLEY BRANCHES

SP's Willamette Valley branch lines date back to 1868. The Wilkins, West Stayton and Newberg branches were once part of a narrow-gauge system that extended from Coburg (near Eugene) all the way to Portland. SP purchased and regauged the Oregonian Railway and the Portland and Willamette Valley narrow gauges in 1890–1893, extending rails south to Springfield and Natron in 1891. A short Springfield–Eugene connection was completed in 1906; it later became part of the Cascade Line.

The West Side Branch between Hillsboro and Eugene was created by the acquisition of the Oregon Central, Western Oregon, Corvallis and Alsea River, and the Portland, Eugene and Eastern built (north to south) between 1868 and 1913. "Red Electric" interurban service operated on the West Side and Newberg branches from 1914 until 1929.

Time and economics have taken their toll on SP's valley branch lines. Most of the old narrow-gauge routes are gone except for the West Stayton and Newberg branches, and a short segment used by the Mill City Branch. The West Side Branch was severed in the 1930s between Monroe and Eugene, and more recently, between Seghers and St. Joseph.

(Left): The Whiteson Turn climbs the 1.92-percent Rex Hill on the Newberg Branch, August 13, 1987. (Above): SD9s and crew take a break at Hillsboro, junction of the West Side and Tillamook Branches, on July 12, 1980.

(Above): There's no business at Suver for the Albany-based "West Side Roustabout" this August 1987 afternoon. (Above right): Willamina and Grande Ronde's S-2 No. 110—former Longview Portland and Northern No. 110—sits at Willamina on August 13, 1987. The 5.5-mile W&GR and a 1.8-mile remnant of the Valley and Siletz Railroad at Independence were purchased by the Willamette Valley Railroad in 1985. (Right): SP's Mill City Local crosses the Santiam River near Lebanon on August 14, 1987. The Mill City Branch was patched togther from portions of the Oregon Pacific, Oregonian narrow gauge and the 1880-built Albany and Lebanon Railroad.

TILLAMOOK BRANCH

By any standard, SP's Tillamook Branch is one of the most stunning examples of railway engineering in the world. It was built in the spirit of territorial madness rather than of necessity, and the result was a right-of-way burdened with endless tunnels, bridges and sharp curves.

Started by William Reid to reach Astoria from Hillsboro, it was halted during the Panic of 1893. In 1905, Harriman interests revived the project, as the Pacific Railway and Navigation Company, designed to keep J.J. Hill's Astoria and Columbia River Railroad from extending south along the coast to Tillamook. Construction of the $5 million PR&N was completed in 1911.

The only shipper of the line today is a paper mill in Tillamook. The Port of Tillamook Bay now leases the entire branch, which makes connections at Hillsboro with a once-weekly SP train from Portland. SP has expressed an interest in selling the line, but if times get much tougher, this most scenic of SP's coast branches will most probably be abandoned.

The Tillamook Branch is famous for its climb over the mountains, but its Pacific Coast trackage is equally scenic. In this view, the Tillamook Hauler heads south along the shores of Nehalem Bay at Wheeler on August 26, 1982.

TOLEDO BRANCH

The Toledo Branch (and the Mill City Branch) are all that remain of Colonel T. Egenton Hogg's Oregon Pacific Railroad, which planned to cross Oregon from Yaquina Bay to a connection with the Oregon Short Line (or a possible extension of the Chicago and Northwestern Railway) in Idaho over a century ago.

Hogg's first attempt, the narrow-gauge Corvallis and Yaquina Bay Railroad, was incorporated in October 1872. Some grading was completed west of Corvallis, but the Panic of 1873 stopped the project. Hogg's standard-gauge Oregon Pacific was organized on September 15, 1880.

The OP reached east from Yaquina Bay to Albany in 1887 and into the Cascades at Idanha in 1890. A small portion of track was laid atop Santiam Pass to secure its passage, but the line was forced into bankruptcy in October 1890. SP purchased the property on July 1, 1915.

Hogg's efforts were not entirely in vain. The U.S. Government built an aircraft spruce mill at Toledo during World War I and today, this Georgia Pacific mill produces enough wood products to make the Toledo Branch SP's most prosperous on the coast.

Ten SD9s, GP40s and TEBU slugs assist another long Toledo Hauler over the 704-foot divide at Summit on June 22, 1984. Ahead lie ten miles of 2.58-percent downgrade.

A long way from Arkansas: Cotton Belt GP40s spliced by SP-built TEBU slugs move 93 cars along the placid Yaquina River near Elk City on August 15, 1987.

COOS BAY BRANCH

The Coos Bay Branch represents SP's third attempt to reach this fine deep water port. The first was the Coos Bay, Roseburg and Eastern Railroad and Navigation Company, incorporated in 1880 to connect Coos Bay with the Oregon and California main line at Roseburg. Twenty-six miles of track between Coos Bay and Myrtle Point were completed before the Panic of 1893 caused construction to stop.

The second attempt, the Oregon Western Railway of 1905, planned to reach Coos Bay from the Siskiyou Line at Drain. Work on it stopped two years later due to yet another economic recession.

When it was learned that J.J. Hill had incorporated the Eugene-Coos Bay Pacific Great Western Railway in 1911, SP reacted by incorporating the Willamette Pacific over the same route. A bargain was soon struck whereby Hill's Oregon Electric would be granted trackage rights over SP's Albany–Lebanon Branch if SP could build its Willamette Pacific. Work on the new line began in 1913 and was completed on August 24, 1916.

Today, Coos Bay Haulers operate every other day from Eugene, and though rumors have persisted that Coos Bay may one day become a coal port, no coal trains have yet to materialize. For the foreseeable future, however, operation of Coos Bay Branch seems secure.

After traversing 50 miles of coastal lowlands (seven miles of it on trestles), the Coos Bay Hauler of September 9, 1979, heads inland along the Siuslaw River at Cushman.

WEYERHAEUSER SPRINGFIELD OPERATIONS

Until 1987, Weyerhaeuser's smallest Northwest logging railroad has been its 22-mile operation east of Springfield. The 13 miles of track between Springfield and Hyland were built by the SP in 1896–1900; the remaining nine miles to Mohawk Transfer were built by Weyerhaeuser in 1960.

SP found itself with a healthy log-hauling business when Weyerhaeuser opened a large pulp and paper mill in Springfield in 1949. Weyerhaeuser began running its own trains on the line in 1960, at which time rails were extended to a new reload at Mohawk Transfer. Because of the 84-ton load restriction on the McKenzie River bridge, Weyerhaeuser acquired a pair of GE 70-tonners from the SP (and later, a pair from British Columbia Hydro). SP stopped running on the line in the early 1960s but Weyerhaeuser log trains lasted another 27 years.

Springfield railroad operations were suspended on August 28, 1987. The rails will soon be removed, erasing forever 90 years of Mohawk Valley railroading.

(Below): A pair of 70-tonners pulls a string of loaded log cars past a longer string of empties at Mohawk Transfer, August 17, 1987. (Right): Two weeks before the line was shut down, a 60-car log train rumbles across the McKenzie River bridge, an 1868 Union Pacific structure which originally spanned the Bear River at Corinne, Utah.

BN's OREGON ELECTRIC

The 132-mile Oregon Electric Railway is one of BN's least known operations, though its tenacity has kept rival SP from completely dominating Willamette Valley for more than 80 years.

The Oregon Electric was incorporated on May 15, 1906, with the intent of constructing an electric interurban line from Portland to Roseburg. J.J. Hill purchased the property in 1908, which became an SP&S subsidiary two years later. Hill had planned to extend the line into California (perhaps to connect with the Sacramento Northern at Chico), but OE rails stopped at Eugene in 1912.

Portland–Eugene interurban trains grew to include parlor and sleeping cars, but a fair amount of freight business developed along the way as well. Passenger service ended in 1933, and the OE was forced to survive the Depression hauling boxcars and flatcars (using home-built electric freight motors for a time and later, diesels).

Under BN management, OE freights continue to operate out of Albany to Sweet Home, Eugene and Portland. Despite a steady business hauling lumber and grass seed, however, BN has recently put the Oregon Electric up for sale.

(Above right): Oregon Electric's Alco tradition—which began with RS-1s in 1945—continued into 1974 with these former NP RS-11s spotted in Eugene. (Right): GP9 No. 1791 and a long string of cars skirt the Willamette River at Albany on August 14, 1987. Due to the miles of street running and the many stops required along the way, the 40-mile trip to Eugene can take as long as 10 hours.

(Right): OE's connections to the outside world are provided by Vancouver (Washington)–Albany train No. 663, seen here rolling through the countryside north of Albany on August 10, 1987. Because of slow running, this 56-car train is already on its second set of crews. (Below): The brakeman and a pair of ex-GN GP9s create a timeless portrait of rural railroading at Millers, where original 1912-era, 75-pound rails are still in use. (Below right): At Junction City (the proposed junction of SP's West Side Branch and Valley Main that never took place), southbound train No. 687 sways down the middle of Holly Street on August 10, 1987. The old OE depot seems to be swaying a bit as well.

Reaching for the Siskiyous

Classic lower quadrant semaphores (such as these at Divide) have long been trademarks of the Siskiyou Branch. The signals were scheduled to be replaced, but SP's recent financial woes have spared their demise.

A FEW MILES SOUTH of Eugene is a place called Springfield Junction, where SP's two California main lines—old and new—diverge. The newer, faster Cascade Line heads southeast toward Klamath Falls, while the older Siskiyou Branch heads south over seven mountain ranges to Ashland and Black Butte. Though bypassed by a majority of the freights, SP's Siskiyou Branch survives on the whims of the lumber business, whose fortunes of late match the grades of the century-old railroad that serves it.

The Siskiyou Branch began life as the southern portion of Ben Holladay's Oregon and California Railroad. Progress on the O&C stopped at Roseburg in 1872, but its new owner, Henry Villard, began pushing rails south again in 1881. By the time the O&C arrived in Ashland three years later, Villard himself was in financial difficulty, and construction over Siskiyou Summit was suspended. The Portland–Ashland line was leased to the Central Pacific in 1887.

Central Pacific, which had been laying rails northward since 1883, soon closed the gap. O&C crews had completed some right-of-way over Siskiyou Summit that kept grades to two percent, but CP chief engineer William Hood decided upon a less expensive route with grades that reached 3.67 percent. The line over Siskiyou Summit was completed in 1887, meeting O&C rails in Ashland on December 16th.

The line's steep grades and unending curves proved an immediate hindrance to operations and profits alike. Though the Siskiyou Line was the first to connect Oregon with California markets, it was not the preferred route of the Central Pacific, whose surveyors had recommended a line via Klamath Falls as early as 1880. Southern Pacific (CP's successor) planned to build this bypass in the early 1900s, but federal antitrust litigation involving E.H. Harriman's UP–SP alliance postponed such action. Most interstate traffic was routed over the Natron Cutoff following its opening in 1926, and the tortuous 300 miles of track that had taken 16 years and three owners to complete soon became a quiet branch line.

Because of its dependence on lumber, the Siskiyou Branch has suffered heavy financial losses in recent years. SP had considered severing the right-of-way between Riddle and Glendale at one time, but because it is part of the so-called "National Rail Defense Network," the entire Siskiyou Branch remains intact. It is heartening to note that this picturesque 300-mile branch line, so well characterized by its Harriman-era semaphore signals, is considered a national resource not only by railfans, but by Uncle Sam as well.

(Above): Oregon, Pacific and Eastern's *Goose* leaves Culp Creek during the summer of 1984 with Mikado No. 19 in charge. (Right): SD45s and SD45T-2s guide a short train through Willow Creek Canyon near Hornbrook, California, on December 23, 1984.

SISKIYOU HOTSHOTS

(Left): A normally elusive (and nocturnal) passage through Cow Creek Canyon, north of Glendale, June 20, 1984. (Below): Three of SP's four experimental TE70-4S "Sulzers" (rebuilt GE U25Bs with Swiss prime movers) roll down Rice Hill on September 12, 1979. The units were later placed in storage at Eugene.

... AND LOCALS

(Below): A portrait of steel bridges, semaphores and SD9s at Drain, September 12, 1979. (Right): The Yoncalla Turn passes through the Oregon countryside north of Drain on July 15, 1980. (Below right): The June 21, 1984 morning lineup at Roseburg with the Sutherlin Local arriving on the right.

CLIMBING THE SISKIYOUS

(Right): Morning light catches a brace of SD45T-2 "tunnel motor" helpers backing down onto a train at Ashland, September 13, 1979. (Below): The U.S. Forest Service requires the use of water cars on trains operating over Siskiyou Summit during dry summer periods. Here, Extra 8311 West climbs the 3.3 percent above Dollarhide with water cars and tunnel motors all working at full blast.

A southbound freight prepares to stop at Siskiyou Summit on December 22, 1984, to check the brakes on a troublesome reefer . . . a wise precaution considering the 3.67-percent downgrade ahead.

NO. 19, THE GOOSE AND THE OP&E

FEW SHORT LINES have been more enjoyable in recent years than the 18-mile Oregon, Pacific and Eastern, which interchanges with the SP at Cottage Grove. Freight service to Culp Creek is as interesting as any, but OP&E's enthusiasm for passengers really set it apart, thanks to a World War I vintage steam locomotive, a bit of scenery, and a lot of style.

OP&E's predecessor, the Oregon and Southeastern Railroad, was built in 1902–1903 to serve the Bohemia gold mines near Culp Creek. The line later extended further into the forests and lumber hauling soon became its dominant business.

The O&SE was reorganized as the Oregon, Pacific and Eastern in 1914. The line changed owners several times over the years and in 1970, was sold to the Row River Investment Company, owned by Bohemia Lumber Company and Kyle Industries.

OP&E president Willis Kyle spent little time in purchasing 2-8-2 No. 19 from the Yreka Western (another Kyle property). Passenger service was

inaugurated on May 1, 1971, with the help of six SP Harriman commute coaches (streamlined cars from the Illinois Central and SP arrived in 1975 and 1979). The train, dubbed the *Goose*, was an immediate success.

Sadly, No. 19 and the *Goose* made their last runs in 1987. Kyle sold his share of the OP&E to the Bohemia Lumber Company, and though over 20,000 people have ridden the *Goose* in recent seasons, Bohemia has proven to be less enthusiastic about tourist operations as was Mr. Kyle. Number 19 was returned to the Yreka Western in May 1988, bringing to an end a very colorful chapter of Oregon railroading.

(Left): OP&E's entire active motive power roster poses at the Cottage Grove shops in 1984. (Above): 2-8-2 No. 19 (Baldwin, 1915) takes care of the weekend tourist business near Dorena on August 25, 1984.

(Above): SW8 No. 602 crosses Bohemia Lumber Mill's wooden arch road-rail bridge at Culp Creek on June 21, 1984. (Right): Steam and scenery along Dorena Lake in 1984.

The Oregon Trunk and the Bend Branch

SOMEWHERE ALONG the Oregon Trunk, Union Pacific's Bend Local will no doubt meet a Burlington Northern train hurrying to or from California. The meet will be amicable, but such was not the case in 1909, when J.J. Hill and E.H. Harriman were hard at work blasting parallel rail lines up the Deschutes Canyon toward the vast range and timber lands of Central Oregon. Though both succeeded at great cost, the so-called "Battle of the Giants" would be the last for Hill and Harriman, and the last frontier railroad war anywhere in America.

Two earlier railroads (the Columbia Southern and the Great Southern) attempted to reach Central Oregon from the Columbia River, but it was obvious that the only reasonable approach was through the rugged Deschutes River Canyon, described in an 1855 War Department survey as "utterly impracticable."

By the turn of the century, however, construction techniques had improved. Union Pacific surveyed a route through the canyon in 1899 (though no construction plans were announced) and in 1906, W.F. "Billy" Nelson incorporated the Oregon Trunk Line, which closely followed the UP survey. With ambitions of reaching California, J.J. Hill sent John F. Stevens to Oregon in 1908 to buy strategic parcels of land and acquire a controlling interest in OT stock (transferred to the SP&S in 1909).

E.H. Harriman reacted by incorporating the Des Chutes Railroad in late 1908. The following summer, Hill had men working along the west bank of the Deschutes River Canyon while Harriman crews worked the east bank, each accusing the other of supply wagon raids, equipment sabotage and gunfire.

Seventy-five miles up the canyon, the OT was forced to use 10 miles of Des Chutes trackage between North Junction and South Junction to avoid crossing the Warm Springs Indian Reservation. The two lines met again near Metolius, where the Des Chutes tracks were forced to stop; it seems that the Oregon Trunk had already secured the only practical crossing of the Crooked River Gorge further south.

A 999-year ceasefire agreement was signed in 1910 and UP's Des Chutes Railroad was granted trackage rights over OT's bridge across the Crooked River Gorge. The following year, UP trackage rights were extended from Redmond to Bend, where Hill drove the last spike on September 6, 1911. (Harriman died in 1909.) The two rivals had spent $25 million to reach a town of only 1,000 people.

Maintaining two separate rights-of-way between the Columbia River and Metolius proved too expensive and in 1923, the Oregon Trunk abandoned its Willow Creek Canyon right-of-way between Metolius and South Junction, securing trackage rights on the UP. Likewise, the UP abandoned its line between North Junction and the Columbia River in 1936, thereby eliminating all duplicate trackage. With only 25 miles of UP's original Des Chutes Railroad still in existence, it was decided to operate the line entirely under Oregon Trunk (and later, BN) operating rules.

The Oregon Trunk, whose charter included an extension to Klamath Falls, applied for permission to do so in 1926. Southern Pacific initially refused to grant trackage rights between Chemult and Klamath Falls, and OT's half owner Northern Pacific later withdrew its support. Undaunted, Great Northern (OT's other owner) applied for approval to build the line (and secure Chemult–Klamath Falls trackage rights) which the ICC granted the following year. GN rails extended south into California where they met the Western Pacific at Bieber in 1931. Though he had passed away 15 years earlier, Hill had, in spirit, finally reached California.

There is one footnote to add: UP's 1982 acquisition of the Western Pacific resulted in an almost all-UP Inside Gateway route between Portland and California (with Bend to Bieber still owned by the SP and BN). Future negotiations with the BN may some day bring about the sale of the Inside Gateway line to the UP.

For if so accomplished, Mr. Harriman will have evened the score.

UP crews give a friendly wave to BN's southbound No. 137 at Metolius, August 28, 1982.

(Above): SP&S RS-3 No. 67 and a GN-style caboose at the Bend engine house, September 23, 1969.

(Above): An Amtrak Deschutes River Excursion climbs along the cliffs above the Columbia River toward the entrance to Deschutes River Canyon on May 15, 1983. (Right): Five GP39-2s pull a southbound Inside Gateway train across Celilo Bridge and the Columbia River, on May 14, 1983. The bridge, completed in 1912, was raised several feet and fitted with a lift span when The Dalles Dam flooded Celilo Falls (over which the bridge was built) in the 1950s.

UP'S BEND LOCAL

Except for local switching around Bend, UP's tri-weekly trip down the "Bend Branch" (UP parlance) is its only remaining operation on "The Trunk" (SP&S parlance).

(Left) SD40-2s take a late afternoon Bend Local across the Deschutes River north of Sherar on July 18, 1980. UP's abandoned Des Chutes Railroad roadbed—now a gravel road—can be seen along the opposite bank. (Below): GP9 No. 310 and GP30 No. 856 make a setout at Maupin, September 23, 1969.

PASSENGER EXTRAS

The Oregon Trunk saw few passenger trains over the years. UP passenger service to Bend was reduced to a mixed train during the Depression as was the SP&S in the 1950s, but the latter survived until the dawning of Amtrak.

(Above): Mishaps jinxed several NRHS-Amtrak Deschutes River excursions; the May 15, 1982 edition (seen here between Sherar and Oakbrook) was no exception. The lead Amtrak unit failed en route and two UP geeps had to be added at The Dalles. (Right): On April 10, 1977, *Coast Starlight* passengers were surprised to find themselves on the Trunk when a derailment closed SP's Cascade Line west of Chemult. Number 13 is seen here approaching OT Junction, four hours late.

BN, Frisco and Western Pacific geeps take train No. 170 across Crooked River Gorge on September 11, 1979. The bridge was the country's second highest when completed in 1911 (SP's original Pecos River bridge, at 321 feet, was a foot higher) and was once featured in Ripley's "Believe It or Not," which claimed that wooden matches dropped from the span caught fire during their descent.

BEYOND BEND

(Right): The 7:00 a.m. lineup at Bend, September 11, 1979: BN freights X27 (with Alco C425 No. 4257) and 147 (with GP30 No. 2231) prepare to head south while UP SD40s await their assignment north to The Dalles. (Below): An hour later, X27 is rolling south near La Pine over former GN rails in full view of Pringle Butte (left), Mount Bachelor, Broken Top and the Three Sisters.

CITY OF PRINEVILLE RAILWAY

Prineville's dreams of becoming a railroad town seemed doomed when Oregon Trunk rails bypassed the town in favor of Bend. Colonel Hogg's Oregon Pacific had intended to pass through Prineville years earlier, but its bankruptcy ended such speculation. Efforts to get the OT to build a branch line into town failed as well.

The Prineville city council decided to take things into its own hands. A $100,000 bond issue was approved in 1916 and by August 1918, the 19-mile City of Prineville Railway had been completed between Prineville and the Oregon Trunk main line near Redmond.

After years of losses, the town's investment began to pay off when nearby national forests opened for harvest in the mid-1930s. Several lumber mills were built in town and by 1942, tonnage was twenty times of that carried in 1935. The railway bonds were paid off in 1960 and three years later, the line was making so much money that all city property taxes were eliminated (later reinstated in the mid-1970s).

Former Milwaukee Road GP9s shuttle cars in and out of lumber mills that keep Prineville's economy alive today. And even if Prineville never became the railroad town it wanted to be, its short line has proven to be well worth the effort.

(Above): After lifting the first half of its train up O'Neil Hill, City of Prineville Alco switchers rumble by Grizzly Mountain to pick up the second half on September 11, 1979. (Below): COP's preference for secondhand equipment included locomotives, rail, bridges and rolling stock. Caboose No. 201 (seen here in 1969) hails from the Lehigh Valley.

(Above): The daily COP freight rolls along the Crooked River Valley countryside a few miles south of Prineville on September 11, 1979. (Left): COP's entire roster ten years earlier: three yellow and black Alco S-1 and S-3 switchers, two cabooses and a former UP coach that residents could ride for free.

Klamath Falls

TO MOST *COAST STARLIGHT* passengers, the town of Klamath Falls is little more than a brief interruption in their passage through Oregon. What escapes the eyes of most Amtrak riders is that "K Falls" is actually a busy rail center served by two Class I railroads and a logging line.

In addition to Southern Pacific's Cascade Line (which handles Amtrak and most of the California–Oregon freight), SP's Modoc Line heads south toward Nevada. Burlington Northern enters town via SP rails from the north and continues south on its own Inside Gateway line to the Union Pacific (formerly Western Pacific) interchange at Bieber. Last but not least is Weyerhaeuser's Oregon, California and Eastern, whose unique EMD-powered U25Bs bring long strings of log cars into town from forests on the other side of Bly Mountain.

The first railroad to reach Klamath Falls was the California Northeastern Railway, formed in 1905 by SP interests. SP acquired the Weed Lumber Company logging railroad (built in 1902–1905) for the California Northeastern and extended it to Klamath Falls in 1909. SP rails continued north of Klamath Falls with the intention of bypassing the Siskiyou Line. Construction of the so-called Natron Cutoff was halted at Kirk in 1911 due to federal SP–UP antitrust litigation.

When the Natron Cutoff was completed in 1926, the fortunes of Klamath Falls began to change. Most Siskiyou Line traffic was rerouted over the new line and Klamath Falls suddenly became a very busy place.

1926 was also the year SP acquired the Nevada–California–Oregon narrow gauge which extended north from Reno to Lakeview, east of Klamath Falls. SP regauged the N-C-O and built a Klamath Falls–Alturas connection (completed in 1929) that created a 210-mile shortcut between Klamath Falls and the East. Though it bypassed the Sierra Nevada Mountains entirely, the new Modoc Line was never very busy; passenger service ended in 1937 and through freight service was suspended in 1987. (SP's new parent Rio Grande reopened the line 21 months later.)

Great Northern arrived in Klamath Falls by way of SP's Natron Cutoff from Chemult in 1928 and continued south to Bieber, where a connection was made with the Western Pacific in 1931. Though initially considered a threat to the SP, the Oregon Trunk–GN–WP "Inside Gateway" route between California and the Northwest never captured more than 20 percent of the business.

It's hard to believe that none of this railroad activity existed until the 1920s, but Klamath Falls is a relative newcomer as railroad towns go. Because of steep grades on SP's Siskiyou Line, GN's California ambitions and vast stands of timber, little "K Falls" has become the second busiest rail center in Oregon.

Southern Pacific SD45T-2 No. 8570 awaits a crew change at the Klamath Falls depot before proceeding south with a California-bound train on June 20, 1984.

(Right): Amtrak's *Coast Starlight* greets the morning sun near Dorris, California, on June 17, 1973. In a few minutes, the train will be stopping in Klamath Falls for servicing and a crew change. (Above left): An Oregon, California and Eastern log train stands idle at "K Falls" during the Christmas 1984 holidays. (Above right): SP&S Alcos and BN geeps prepare to leave town on the Inside Gateway to California, June 16, 1973.

(Left): SP's southbound BRLAT (Brooklyn-Los Angeles Trailers) hustles into Klamath Falls on July 17, 1980. (Above): The blue "Men at Work" sign is removed from a freight departing the SP yards in June 1984 as a Modoc Line freight arrives from Nevada.

K FALLS IN WINTER, DECEMBER 29, 1984

(Right): Oblivious to the falling snow, SD9E No. 4405 switches the Alturas Local at Lost River on the Modoc Line. (Below right): A southbound Cascade Line freight rolls through Texum, northern terminus of the Modoc Line (foreground).

WEYERHAEUSER AND THE OC&E

The Oregon, California and Eastern Railway was incorporated by Robert Strahorn in 1915 as a proposed network of lines connecting Klamath Falls with Bend, Prineville, Burns and Lakeview. Strahorn, who had constructed UP's North Coast Railway between Spokane, Pasco and Yakima and later managed the Portland, Eugene and Eastern in the Willamette Valley, convinced the City of Klamath Falls to finance his venture in 1916.

The line had little difficulty completing the first 20 miles of track to Dairy, but the route north over Bly Mountain required an ascent of nearly 1,000 feet on a 2.6-percent grade. Though a 1,300-foot tunnel had been planned, a pair of switchbacks was constructed over the summit instead. Crossing Bly Mountain and his purchase of Klamath Falls' share of the enterprise in 1919 took the last of Strahorn's money, and the OC&E was forced to stop at Sprague River in 1923. Several independent logging lines in the area kept the OC&E in business until SP purchased the line in 1927. A year later, Great Northern purchased a half interest and rails were extended east to Bly. Though the OC&E continued to operate independently, SP and GN began operating the line directly on alternate years (and later, five-year periods) in 1933.

Weyerhaeuser's "Woods Line" was built in 1940–1941 to reach the forests north of Sycan, so it seemed appropriate when Weyerhaeuser (which owns a sprawling mill complex in Klamath Falls) bought the OC&E in 1975. Leased SP locomotives were used initially, but it was the 1976 arrival of odd-sounding, EMD-powered U25Bs that gave the OC&E its unique personality, still very much in evidence today.

(Above left): Morrison-Knudsen TE53-1-4Es on Bly Mountain Pass, once frequented by SP cab-forward 2-8-8-2s. (Left): Baldwin RS12s Nos. 7908 and 7909 (Seaboard Coast Line units purchased in 1977) switch empties at the BN interchange yard east of Klamath Falls on July 17, 1980.

BLY MOUNTAIN

(Above): A 50-car log train backs into East Switchback on August 24, 1982. (Right): Ten minutes later, the train is moving forward again, navigating the horseshoe curve below East Switchback on the 2.62-percent descent into Dairy.

THE "WOODS LINE"

(Above left): Two former BN GP9s and a former OC&E U-boat switch skeleton log cars at Sycan on June 20, 1984. The geeps and the reidentified U-boat replaced four Baldwin switchers purchased in 1950–1951. (Left): Inside the shops at Sycan.

BN's INSIDE GATEWAY

The Oregon Trunk proposed building a line from Bend to the OC&E railhead at Sprague River via Silver Lake (one of Strahorn's planned extensions) in 1926, but a year later it was the Great Northern that purchased a half share of the OC&E and secured Chemult–Klamath Falls trackage rights over the SP. The latter turned out to be the better option, for GN would certainly have been forced to construct a tunnel beneath OC&E's Bly Mountain switchbacks, an expensive proposition to say the least. GN rails continued south to Bieber and the Western Pacific in 1931, creating the Inside Gateway and some competition for the Southern Pacific.

(Right): At Bieber, California, 91 miles south of Klamath Falls, a BN train begins its northward journey on December 28, 1984, while UP units await fresh crews for the next train south.

(Below): A GN GP35 and BN Alco C636 rest between assignments at BN's Klamath Falls Yard, June 16, 1973. (Below right): A BN Inside Gateway freight climbs the 0.8-percent of SP's Calimus Hill near Chiloquin on June 19, 1984.

SP's Natron Cutoff

Amtrak's *Coast Starlight* poses at McCredie Springs with a collection of former Santa Fe coaches and Pullmans in tow, July 16, 1980.

THE STORY OF SP's Natron Cutoff is as much a study of persistence as it is about railroad building. The 275-mile line took 21 years to complete; it wasn't economics or mountain ranges that took so long, but two controversial U.S. Supreme Court decisions and a world war.

In the early years of SP's Siskiyou Line operations, it was actually faster to travel between San Francisco and Oregon by steamship than by rail. Plans to bypass the Siskiyou Line began during the summer of 1905 when UP–SP boss E.H. Harriman incorporated the Oregon Eastern Railway and the California Northeastern Railway. The OE planned to connect the SP main line in Eugene with the UP main line on the Idaho border via Cascade Summit. By building a branch of the OE from Chemult to Klamath Falls (where it would connect with the California and Northeastern extending northward from the Siskiyou Line), a bypass of the Siskiyou Line could be achieved.

Construction of the Oregon Eastern began at both Natron (near Springfield) and Klamath Falls, but was halted on May 1, 1912, due to the loss of a lengthy battle against the 1908 U.S. Supreme Court decision to split up the UP–SP alliance. To further complicate matters, the Supreme Court later ruled that SP's acquisition of the Central Pacific (under which all SP Oregon lines operated) was illegal.

World War I intervened and it wasn't until 1923 that the ICC and the Justice Department gave SP permission to keep the Central Pacific. The ICC granted approval to resume work on the 118-mile gap between Kirk and Oakridge on August 15, 1923, and construction resumed almost immediately.

Tracklaying between Kirk and Cascade Summit was relatively easy, but the remaining 61 miles which lay on the steep western slopes of the Cascades was quite a different matter. In its 44-mile, 3,700-foot descent into Oakridge, the line required the construction of 19 tunnels, 10 snowsheds and several large steel bridges. Three thousand workers took two years to complete the job, which cost nearly $25 million more than budgeted.

Special trains from Portland and San Francisco met a few miles east of Oakridge where the final spike was driven home on August 7, 1926. Though only 24 miles shorter than the Siskiyou Line, the new "Cascade

Line" eliminated 51 complete circles of curvature and 2,870 feet of cumulative ascent while reducing maximum grades from 3.67 to 1.8 percent. Passenger train schedules were 3½ hours faster than comparable Siskiyou Line running times and freight traffic enjoyed similar improvements.

Such improvements did little to withstand the forces of nature in 1964. On a stormy December 22nd, an avalanche struck a freight train near Frasier, tumbling five freight cars down the mountainside. A second avalanche followed moments later, taking with it 100 feet of track. Before the 21-day storm subsided, a 130-foot section of Noisy Creek Bridge washed away and 700 feet of roadbed near Oakridge was smothered by a mudslide. The multimillion-dollar repairs took 17 days to complete.

On July 17, 1980, a northbound freight ("eastbound" to the SP) roars through Kirk, where construction of the Natron Cutoff stalled for nearly 12 years.

Winters have been gentler since, and tunnel motor SD45T-2s and Superliners now frequent the rails once dominated by cab-forward articulateds and *Shasta Daylights*. Though SP's Cascade Line was one of the longest, most costly line relocations in American history, it has proven to be a sound investment for both the Southern Pacific and Oregon.

CHEMULT

(Left): It's June and it's snowing as FP7 No. 6459 and two SDP45s pull a long northbound *Starlight* out of Chemult in 1973. (Below left): Chemult became a railroad junction when the Great Northern arrived from Bend in 1927. In this August 24, 1982 view, BN's No. 170 from Klamath Falls leaves the joint SP–BN trackage on its northward journey to Bend.

CASCADE SUMMIT

Though 4,885-foot Cascade Summit holds the distinction of being the highest railroad pass in the Cascade Mountains, it is not the highest point on the Cascade Line. That distinction belongs to 5,063-foot Grass Lake Summit in California.

(Above): Helpers (foreground) watch freights meet at the east switch of Cascade Summit siding on a foggy April morning in 1977. (Right): The northbound *Coast Starlight* crests the summit on May 26, 1974, an early morning tradition that began with the all-Pullman *Cascade* in 1927.

"THE HILL"—44 MILES OF 1.7 PERCENT GRADE

(Above): There's still plenty of snow at Cruzatte (elevation 4,100 feet) as a freight works its way toward Cascade Summit on May 16, 1980. (Right): A work train crosses a ravine wedged between Tunnels 7 and 8 north of Cruzatte, August 25, 1982.

(Above): Amidst a blaze of wildflowers, a lone SD45T-2 drifts across Salt Creek trestle on its way to Oakridge, July 16, 1980. (Right): Five SD9s roar up the winding grade between Pryor and McCredie Springs with a long string of boxcars. The old gals, which work Willamette Valley locals during the week, are often used as helpers on weekends; on this August 1987 afternoon, they got the starring role.

EUGENE TO OAKRIDGE

(Above left): A water skier paces a Klamath Falls-bound freight along Lookout Point reservoir near Crale on July 16, 1980. Completion of the reservoir in 1954 required relocating 21 miles of SP's main line. (Above): Helpers are added to upgrade trains anywhere between Natron and Oakridge. Here at Dougren in May 1981, the head end adds a single SD45T-2 for the long climb ahead. (Left): Just after the local switcher has tied up for the night, SP No. 11, the southbound *Coast Starlight,* rolls by the Springfield depot on the evening of July 15, 1980.

KLAMATH NORTHERN RAILWAY

Completed in 1938, the Klamath Northern Railway extends 10.6 miles north from Gilchrist Junction on the SP main line to serve the Gilchrist Timber Company mill, which owns the line. Trains run as required (generally twice weekly), and college kids maintain the roadbed during the summer months.

(Above): A KN freight bounces over 68-pound rail with five cars bound for Gilchrist Junction on August 25, 1982. GE 70-tonner No. 205 has since been supplemented by GE 125-tonner No. 207, delivered in December 1982. (Right): Top speed (20 mph) from the engineer's point of view.

Blue Mountains Suite

WEDGED BETWEEN the Snake and Columbia Rivers in northeast Oregon is a series of ridges known as the Blue Mountains. It was through this rugged region that 19th-century pioneers followed the Oregon Trail; so too did railroad builders a generation later, creating the Northwest's second transcontinental route in the process.

Union Pacific's Blue Mountains main line began as an extension of the Oregon Railway and Navigation built in 1882–1884. Soon after Henry Villard formed the OR&N in 1879, an agreement was made with the UP to connect OR&N's Columbia River line to UP's main line in Wyoming. The two were to meet at Baker City (now Baker), Oregon, but no construction took place for several years.

As the Northern Pacific transcontinental neared completion, UP feared it might lose its best chance to reach the Northwest. Renewed discussions with the OR&N resulted in the incorporation of UP's Oregon Short Line in 1881, chartered to extend west from Granger, Wyoming, to Baker City (and, if necessary, all the way to the Pacific).

Construction on what was known as OR&N's "Baker City Branch" began at Umatilla in March 1881. Throughout the next 18 months, rela-

tions between the OR&N and the UP deteriorated as both threatened to extend beyond Baker City with its own line. In September 1882, Villard sent surveyors into the narrow Burnt River Canyon east of Baker City with the intent of reaching Boise and keeping the UP out of Oregon. At a meeting the following February, however, the two rivals agreed to join rails at Huntington, a few miles west of the Oregon–Idaho border.

The OR&N reached Pendleton on August 31, 1882. Further east, the right-of-way was located over an 1868–1869 UP survey, crossing three ridges in the process: 4,205-foot Kamela, 3,448-foot Telocaset and 3,968-foot Encina. Baker City was reached in August 1884, and on November 25, 1884, the last spike was driven at Huntington.

UP acquired control of the OR&N in 1887, resulting in an all-UP route between Omaha and the Northwest. Subsequent completion of lines to Seattle, Yakima, Spokane and Bend made the Blue Mountains district UP's busiest in the Northwest, and at times a frustrating bottleneck.

To ease the congestion, most of the trackage between Hinkle and Pendleton was rebuilt between 1902 and 1914 and a second track was added across Kamela Summit in 1917–1918. Locomotive and yard facilities at Umatilla and Rieth were moved to Hinkle in 1951 to accommodate the construction of McNary Dam on the Columbia River. Stories about bypassing Kamela Summit with a long tunnel have been around for a long time, but such an undertaking has always been considered too expensive.

Perhaps the best way to view the Blue Mountains—and UP's attempt to conquer them—is from a window seat on Amtrak's *Pioneer*. Though steam, E units and DDA40Xs are now only memories, UP's Blue Mountains operations are still an impressive enterprise.

UP's famous FEF-3 class Northern No. 8444 rolls through Thorn Hollow with an all first-class Oregon Historical Society special on September 15, 1979.

(Above): A matched A-B-B-A set of E9s is in charge of this Portland-bound *Old Timers Special* at Nordeen on April 20, 1979. (Left): "Trucking on down" Durkee Loop, August 21, 1982.

(Left): That's not just anybody's business car spotted in front of the 1930s' era brick depot on August 22, 1982—No. 101 belongs to UP's then-Chairman of the Board, John Kenefick. (Below): The morning lineup at La Grande, June 9, 1977: SD24 helpers, a pair of westbound freights and an eastbound powered by two *Centennials* and a "fast forty" (89 mph geared) SD40-2. It looks like a promising day.

LA GRANDE

Soon after the first OR&N train arrived in 1884, La Grande moved its entire business district alongside the railroad. The town became a division point in 1913, constructing large shops and a 34-stall roundhouse in the process.

WINTER IN THE BLUES, 1978

(Above): Amtrak's *Pioneer* seems to be flying through the snow at Rieth on March 4, 1978. (Right): The following day, westbound symbol freight PSV-3 (Portland–Seattle Vans) was spotted at Nordeen, on the climb to 4,205-foot Kamela Summit.

EAST OF LA GRANDE

(Above): Amtrak's *Pioneer* meets a string of SD45s in the hole at Telocaset on June 9, 1977. (Above left): Two DDA40Xs and an SD40-2 bring the westbound OMN (Overland Mail Northwest) over Telocaset Hill two days later. (Left): Telocaset Hill caused the OR&N to miss Union, so the town built its own railroad, the Central Railway of Oregon, to the OR&N main line in 1890. The Union Railroad of Oregon purchased the property in 1927, whose two tiny Plymouth diesels are seen here at Union on August 22, 1982.

(Opposite page): Seven SD40-2s (three on the point, four mid-train) take a long westbound drag up the 2.2-percent grade at Durkee Loop on June 16, 1984.

ALONG THE JOSEPH BRANCH

The 83.7-mile Joseph Branch was built in two sections: La Grande to Elgin in 1890 by the Oregon Railway Extensions Company, and Elgin to Joseph in 1905–1908 by the OR&N. UP operates trains over the branch three times a week on a leisurely one day up/next day back schedule.

(Above): A late afternoon view of the Joseph Local along the Wallowa River near Minam, June 17, 1984. (Left): UP's Elgin depot still sported steam-era white and green paint and a train order semaphore in this 1984 view; the structure has since been sold to the city.

REBUILDING THE SUMPTER VALLEY LEGEND

The Sumpter Valley Railway found itself in the midst of a gold rush soon after it reached the town of Sumpter in 1896, but it was timber that sustained the legendary little narrow gauge until its abandonment in 1947.

A group of railfans began rebuilding the line from McEwen (renamed Dredge) to Sumpter in the early 1970s. Tourist operations began on July 3, 1976, and continue today during the summer months.

(Below): A view of the property at Dredge in 1982. Standard-gauge ties donated by the UP are readily apparent. (Right): Caboose No. 5, built in 1926, is one of the few SV cars and locomotives still in existence. (Below right): A latter-day SV passenger train, with Eccles Lumber Company Heisler No. 3 in charge of two open-air cars built from Rio Grande gondolas. Eccles Lumber Company was a feeder line to the Sumpter Valley.

Tracks Across the Desert

After wyeing the geep and caboose, the UP crew this August 20, 1982 morning will pick up 25 loads at the Oregon and Northwestern interchange in Hines, then head across the desert to Nampa, Idaho.

SOUTH OF THE Blue Mountains and east of Bend lies a part of Oregon not well known to outsiders, a vast inland desert that extends into Nevada. Only along the Malheur (French for "bad hour," or misfortune) River flowing east toward Idaho did railroad builders find any potential for business. The result of their efforts was UP's Oregon Eastern Branch, 157 miles of railroad that traverses the barren, hostile landscape from Ontario to Burns.

There were several plans to build across the desert, though only two were ever attempted. The first was Colonel T. Egenton Hogg's Oregon Pacific, promoted as a line extending from Yaquina Bay on the coast to Prineville, Burns and the Oregon Short Line in Ontario (or a possible connection to the Chicago and Northwestern Railway further east). Hogg managed to build 155 miles of track from the coast to the Cascades and 12 miles of grade in Malheur Canyon by 1889, but the road declared bankruptcy the following year and no further progress was made.

The Malheur Valley Railway commenced construction from the UP main line at Ontario to Vale in 1906. Rails pushed west of Vale in 1912 as part of the Oregon Eastern Railway, a proposed joint UP–SP network which was to extend from Ontario to Eugene and Klamath Falls. The U.S. Supreme Court split up the UP–SP alliance in 1913, and the Oregon Eastern project was subsequently abandoned.

Under UP–Oregon Short Line ownership, the Oregon Eastern reached Burns in 1924 to serve nearby timberlands opened by the U.S. Forest Service. Though no further construction was undertaken, the resulting Oregon Eastern Branch survived on agriculture and connections with the Oregon and Northwestern Railroad at Burns. Business through the desert lands west of Vale gradually became more dependent on the O&NW interchange and the Hines Lumber Company mill in Hines.

In March 1984, however, Mother Nature intervened when unusually wet weather caused Malheur Lake to flood the surrounding region, including several miles of the Oregon Eastern Branch, which cut off rail service to Burns and the O&NW. UP's last run from Burns was made on March 8th.

Portions of the line remained submerged until 1987 when the Oregon Eastern Branch was sold to Western Intermountain Industries of Boise. The sale, however, was never consummated and in 1989, the line was acquired by the Wyoming Colorado Railroad, which plans to raise UP's soggy roadbed above flood stage with the help of county, state and federal funds.

At long last, it appears that trains will make tracks across the desert once again.

The August 22, 1982 Burns Local crosses the Malheur River just east of Juntura with an almost solid block of Oregon and Northwestern boxcars. The Oregon Eastern Branch was part of UP's Idaho Division and as such, operated on Mountain Time.

OREGON AND NORTHWESTERN RAILROAD

The 50-mile Oregon and Northwestern began life as the Malheur Railroad, proposed in the early 1920s by Fred Herrick to fulfill a condition to harvest timber in the Ochoco and Malheur National Forests. In anticipation of the new business, UP extended its Oregon Eastern Branch from Crane to Burns in 1924.

Little was accomplished on the Malheur Railroad until the Edward Hines Western Pine Company bought the property in 1928, renaming it the Oregon and Northwestern Railroad. The O&NW was constructed in 1928–1929 between Burns and Seneca, where a mill and network of logging railroads were soon built. A succession of secondhand Consolidation and Mikado steam locomotives kept the line running until 1955, when Baldwin's AS-616 diesel demonstrator No. 1600 arrived. Two Alco S-3s were purchased in 1956, but were replaced by three more Baldwin AS-616s acquired from the SP and McCloud River Railroad in 1966 and 1970, giving the O&NW the distinction of being an all-Baldwin enterprise.

Operations to Seneca dwindled to one train per week in later years. The March 6, 1984, train proved to be the last before the Malheur Lake floods shut down UP's Oregon Eastern Branch, O&NW's only connection to the outside world.

Since then, the planing mill in Seneca has moved to John Day, and Hines Lumber Company has sold its holdings (including the O&NW) to the Snow Mountain Pine Company Thus, when the Oregon Eastern Branch reopens, all but a few miles of the O&NW will be abandoned. In the interim, O&NW's four big Baldwins sit silently in Hines, awaiting an uncertain fate.

(Above): O&NW Baldwin AS-616 No. 4 (former McCloud River Railroad No. 34) puts on a show as it climbs the 2.7-percent grade through Poison Creek Canyon on August 23, 1982. (Right): Switching the mill at Hines.

(Above): O&NW's weekly train to Seneca crosses the Silvies River a few miles south of Seneca on August 23, 1982. (Right): Modern 50-foot double-door boxcars share duties with ancient, water barrel-equipped flats whose age, by their own admission, is "over 50" (above right).

A 4449 Album

THE DIESEL AGE has not been kind to most steam locomotives. Those that escaped the cutter's torch have usually ended up in parks or fairgrounds as static displays. Such was certainly the case of 4449, a 1941 example of streamlined steam built by the Lima Locomotive Works for Southern Pacific's glamorous *Daylight* fleet. 4449 was donated to the City of Portland in 1958 and moved to Oaks Park where she sat for 16 years, devoid of her streamlined skirts, looking forlorn and forgotten.

On December 14, 1974, however, an extraordinary event occurred. 4449 was towed from Oaks Park to Burlington Northern's Hoyt Street roundhouse for a four-month, $400,000 overhaul. Completely rebuilt and sporting bicentennial red, white and blue livery, the "Pride of Portland" left for Chicago on June 20, 1975, for an appointment with the American Freedom Train tour.

4449 returned to Portland with Amtrak's *Transcontinental Steam Excursion* in 1977 and was placed in storage at UP's Albina shops, hidden from public view for nearly four years. In 1981, 4449 was invited to attend the opening ceremonies of the California State Railroad Museum in Sacramento and thanks to the SP and the Pacific Northwest Chapter of the National Railway Historical Society, the patriotic AFT red, white and blue paint was removed in favor of *Daylight* red and orange (much to the relief of purists). Following a test run to Eugene, 4449 left for Sacramento with a 15-car excursion train. Unfortunately, a flue tube ruptured on the return leg of the journey and excursionists were forced to complete the trip behind a pair of decidedly non-art deco SD45T-2s.

But 4449 would be back . . . in style. At the invitation of the New Orleans World's Fair, 4449 steamed out of Portland on May 5, 1984, with the *Louisiana World's Fair Daylight*.

Since then, 4449 has made a trip to Hollywood in 1986 to star in the Disney movie, *Tough Guys,* and pulled SP&S 4-8-4 No. 700 (another Oaks Park resident) to Portland's 1987 Railroad Fair.

High operating and insurance costs prevent 4449 from running with any predictable frequency these days. Though currently stored at SP's Brooklyn roundhouse, it's doubtful 4449 will ever return to Oaks Park . . . her fans would never allow it.

A fresh mantle of snow greets Extra 4449 East at Cascade Summit, returning home a movie star with the "Disney Daylight" on April 16, 1986.

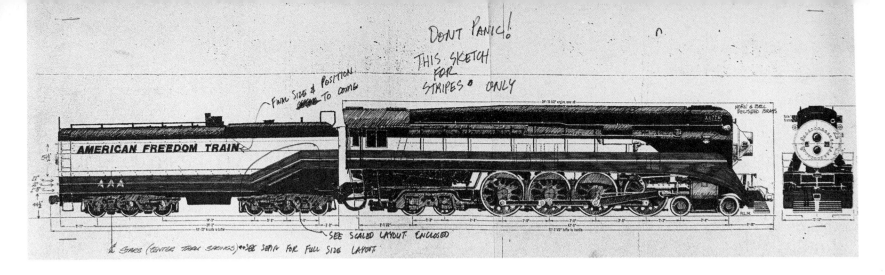

DON'T PANIC!
THIS SKETCH FOR STRIPES ONLY

AMERICAN FREEDOM TRAIN

(Above): Painting-lettering sketch of the red, white and blue American Freedom Train color scheme. (Left): With only a coat of black paint applied so far, a reborn 4449 builds up steam at Hoyt Street. Though taken April 26, 1975, the scene appears timeless. (Below): SP 4449 greets the Oregon City local at Coalca on the April 7, 1981, test run to Eugene.

(Opposite page): Whistle blowing and rods flashing, 4449 and the *Louisiana World's Fair Daylight* glide along the shores of Grass Lake, California, on May 6, 1984. Can there be any doubt why SP considered its *Daylight* "The Most Beautiful Train in the World"?

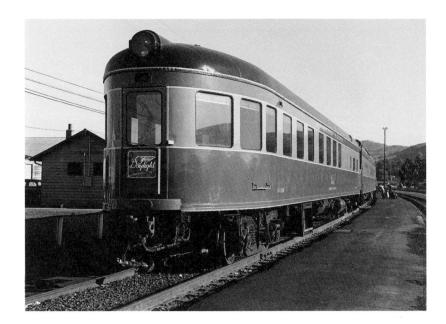

(Below): From the teardrop-shaped exhaust stack and classification lights to the chrome-striped pilot, SP's streamlined GS-class Northerns were considered by many to be the most beautiful ever built. (Right): Even if Great Northern's "Appekunny Mountain" did pinch hit for a proper *Daylight* observation car, its neon drumhead and red-orange-black livery seen here on the rear of the *Louisiana World's Fair Daylight* brought back a flood of memories to those lucky enough to have witnessed "The Real Thing."

(Below right): The glory and power of Lima Superpower is readily apparent in this mile-a-minute portrait taken along the SP main line north of Eugene.

Idaho Panhandle

Sunrise on the Camas Prairie (and the Grangeville Local) at Cottonwood, September 9, 1978.

(Opposite page): A westbound Milwaukee Road freight crosses Benewah Viaduct west of St. Maries on September 10, 1978. This scenic portion of the Milwaukee was often overlooked by railfans who preferred the more famous electrified divisions to the east and west.

THERE ARE ACTUALLY two Idahos: the arid southern portion, and the smaller, more scenic northern portion known as the Panhandle. The two are divided by the rugged wilderness of the Salmon River ("River of No Return"), which is also the boundary between the Pacific and Mountain time zones in the state.

Unlike the Union Pacific-dominated southern half, the Panhandle is traversed by several transcontinental rail lines, branch lines and short lines (as well as the Camas Prairie Railroad, which is difficult to categorize as

either branch line or short line). Certainly geography had much to do with this profusion of railroads, but so too did the state's timber, grain and mineral resources that lured railroad builders into the mountains and the prairies.

Idaho railroading never gets busier than it does at Sandpoint, where three transcontinental main lines converge. Beyond the constant procession of BN freights, there are UP's Spokane International trains to and from Canada, Amtrak *Empire Builders* and newcomer Montana Rail Link. Even the Pend Oreille Valley Railroad, located in the northeast corner of Washington State, depends on BN's Newport–Sandpoint rails for connections to the outside world.

The discovery of gold brought legions of miners into the mountains east of Coeur d'Alene in the 1880s. Daniel C. Corbin was the first to build rails there (in 1887). Later, a UP branch from Washington and an NP branch from Montana created an unintentional trans-Idaho route which for a few frantic days in 1892 hosted NP transcontinental traffic after a bridge collapsed on the main line at Hope. During the next 90-odd years, however, the railroads have kept busy transporting gold, silver and lead from one of the richest mining districts in the country.

The Milwaukee Road located its Idaho Division main line along the St. Joe River and Coeur d'Alene Lake (parts of which are now operated by the St. Maries River Railroad). The unelectrified "gap" created between the electrified Rocky Mountain and Coast divisions was often ignored by railfans; ironically, more Idaho Division trackage has survived than either of its more famous neighbors.

The southernmost rail operation in the Panhandle is the Camas Prairie Railroad, arguably the best-known branch line in the Northwest. From its Lewiston headquarters, the UP and NP (now BN) have operated the Camas Prairie harmoniously and productively under a unique joint arrangement forged in 1909. As with the St. Maries River Railroad further north, timber giant Potlatch provides the necessary resources to keep the Camas Prairie alive today.

It's amazing how much railroading has been built into a space barely 50 miles wide and 200 miles long. Certainly the 90 minutes it takes to traverse the Panhandle is much too brief; the scenic route from Canada to the Camas Prairie, however, is highly recommended.

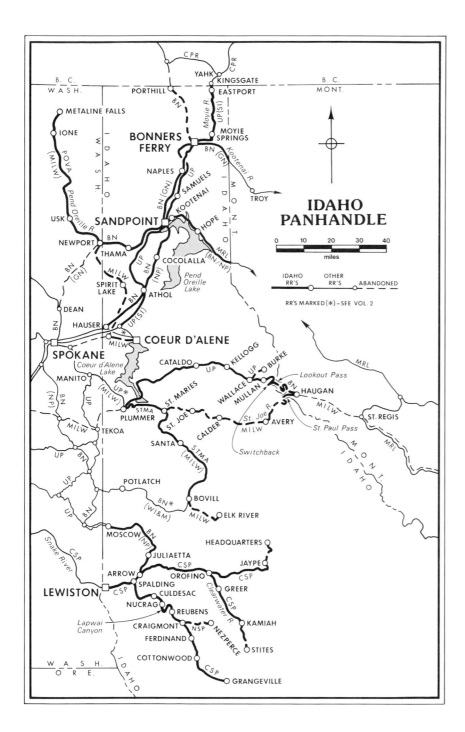

IDAHO PANHANDLE

0 10 20 30 40
miles

IDAHO   OTHER
RR'S   RR'S   ABANDONED

RR'S MARKED (✳) — SEE VOL. 2

Spokane International train No. 9, powered by pooled CP Rail SD40-2s this September 11, 1978 morning, waits to clear U.S. Customs at the border town of Eastport before leaving for Spokane.

(Right): UP's Kellogg Local rounds a curve along the shores of Coeur d'Alene Lake at Shingle Bay on July 28, 1983. (Below): St. Maries River Railroad's Avery Logger at Avery, July 23, 1983. (Below right): On a June afternoon in 1979, BN train No. 84 (foreground) has taken the siding at Naples to meet the flagship of the fleet, No. 3, whose ancestors have included the *Pacific Fast Mail* and more recently, the *Pacific Zip*.

Rails Through Sandpoint

SANDPOINT MAY BE better known as a resort town, but with three busy railroad main lines passing through, it qualifies as a railroad town as well. BN's former Northern Pacific main line arrives from Spokane by way of a long viaduct across Lake Pend Oreille, swinging east along the Clark Fork into Montana. Union Pacific's Spokane International and the former Great Northern Spokane main line enter Sandpoint along the Pend Oreille River and continue their parallel paths north to Bonners Ferry and beyond.

The ghost of Milwaukee Road's Spokane–Metaline Falls branch (nee Idaho and Washington Northern Railroad) plays a part as well. Though its right-of-way south of Newport was abandoned in 1976, the Newport–Metaline Falls (Washington) segment still exists thanks to a unique county Port Authority arrangement which took over the operation on October 1, 1979. Connections to Sandpoint are made via BN's Newport Local.

In addition to BN's mainline freights (and nocturnal *Empire Builders*), there are Montana Rail Link trains, BN locals to Newport, Bonners Ferry and Troy, and UP freights to and from Canada.

Needless to say, the rails through Sandpoint are kept well polished.

Symbol freight SPH enters Idaho territory on BN's busy Spokane–Sandpoint main line, June 23, 1983.

BN OPERATIONS

Sandpoint's first railroad was the Northern Pacific, completed through Idaho in 1882. A division point and engine servicing facilities were originally established at Hope, but moved west to Kootenai in 1909, where a 20-stall roundhouse, coal dock and car shops were built.

Great Northern construction crews passed through Sandpoint in 1892, moving eastward to Troy, where tracks extending westward from Kalispell were met later that year. GN made extensive use of the NP at Sandpoint for the shipment of construction materials.

Operations through Sandpoint changed considerably after the 1970 BN merger. Most BN transcontinental traffic soon shifted to the former NP main line south of Sandpoint and to the former GN main line north of Sandpoint. New connecting tracks in Spokane and Sandpoint were completed in December 1972 at a cost of $19 million. The NP line east to Missoula remained active, but GN's line west to Spokane didn't fare as well: the center Dean–Newport segment was abandoned in 1984 (though Spokane–Dean–Kettle Falls and Sandpoint–Newport locals continue to operate over the remaining portions).

The arrival of Montana Rail Link in 1987 opens a new chapter of Sandpoint area railroading that began with Northern Pacific 4-4-0s a century ago. However the story unfolds, it will be well worth watching.

(Above): Pend Oreille Valley's Alco RS-32 No. 102 chugs across a trestle south of Ione, Washington, with cars bound for Newport and Sandpoint on August 6, 1981. (Right): A westbound Spokane International grain extra passes through downtown Bonners Ferry on March 21, 1987.

SOUTH TO SPOKANE

Because of its superior alignment, NP's right-of-way was chosen over the Great Northern's as BN's primary Spokane–Sandpoint main line. Traffic has become so heavy that BN has considered adding a second track. Two trains spotted on June 2, 1979, included a westbound extra at Cocolalla (right) powered by an SD24 and two U25Cs (all Burlington alumni) and an eastbound train crossing the 4,769-foot Pend Oreille Viaduct (opposite page), NP's southern entry into Sandpoint.

(Below): BN train No. 104 rolls through the snowy Idaho landscape north of Athol on February 9, 1985. This portion of NP right-of-way was relocated in 1900 and again in 1965, when the massive fill in the background helped eliminate a long trestle, a tunnel and 1.82 miles of track.

A leased Denver and Rio Grande SD45 assists two BN SD40-2s with train No. 196 over Pack River Viaduct near Hope on June 25, 1987.

EAST TO HOPE AND PARADISE

The former NP main line follows the north shore of Lake Pend Oreille to the mouth of the Clark Fork (one of the few rivers named "Fork" rather than "River" or "Creek"), which provides a water level passage to Garrison, 286 miles further east. This portion of BN's Rocky Mountain Division was leased to Montana Rail Link in 1987 and no longer sees BN-operated freights or (since 1979) Amtrak's *North Coast Hiawatha*.

NORTH TO BONNERS FERRY

GN's main line was built north from Sandpoint to Bonners Ferry in 1892, then headed east along the Kootenai River Canyon into Montana. A five-mile line relocation was built between Deep Creek and Naples around the turn of the century; the older alignment was adopted by the Spokane International a few years later.

Beneath a backdrop of the Selkirk Mountains, eastbound BN container train No. 14 hustles through Bonners Ferry on the first day of Spring 1987.

AT THE CROSSROADS IN SANDPOINT

(Right): Eastbound SDs and double stacks cross Sand Creek and the Spokane International main line at Boyer on March 21, 1987. Boyer siding was created as part of the 1972 NP–GN main line connection project and forms the boundary between Boyer East and Boyer West dispatchers. (Below right): The NP-built depot sports "Sandpoint" signs borrowed from the GN depot west of town. (Below): Train No. 75 from Missoula makes a brief stop for radiator water at Sandpoint Junction on June 2, 1979.

WEST TO NEWPORT

GN's Sandpoint–Spokane main line was relegated to secondary status after the BN merger and severed in 1984 when rails between Dean and Newport were abandoned. Today, only a local to Newport roams the Idaho portion of the main line that once hosted incomparable *Empire Builders*.

A day with the Newport Local, August 21, 1986. (Above): Approaching GN-style semaphores at Thama. (Left): Heading home from Newport with a string of cement hoppers from the Pend Oreille Valley Railroad. It's always nice to see former GN geeps on GN rails, but GP30 No. 2200 died earlier that morning, leaving GP9 No. 1764 to finish the day's chores.

PEND OREILLE VALLEY RAILROAD

For generations, residents of Pend Oreille County in northeast Washington have depended on Milwaukee Road's Spokane–Metaline Falls branch for the transportation of its cement and lumber products. When it seemed certain that Milwaukee operations in the area were doomed, the local populace sprang into action, creating (in 1979) the state's only Port District dedicated solely to the operation of a railroad. The result—with the help of $3.2 million in federal grants—was the 61.5-mile Pend Oreille Valley Railroad.

The line was built by the Idaho and Washington Northern Railroad which reached Metaline Falls from Spokane via Spirit Lake, Idaho, in 1911. Milwaukee Road purchased the property in 1916 and continued to operate it until October 1, 1979. The right-of-way south of Newport was abandoned in 1976, at which time Milwaukee obtained trackage rights over the former GN main line between Spokane and Newport.

Pend Oreille Valley traffic has increased steadily over the years due to the cement plant in Metaline Falls and the recent opening of a newsprint mill at Usk. The future of the POVA appears secure, thanks to the citizens of Pend Oreille County.

(Below): Initially operated with leased Kyle Railways Alcos, the Pend Oreille Valley currently owns a pair of former BN GP9s. Red and gray No. 101 is seen here at Metaline Falls on August 25, 1988. (Right): In its early days, POVA traffic out of Metaline Falls was often a bit light, as suggested by this view taken at Box Canyon in August 1981.

UP'S SPOKANE INTERNATIONAL

Union Pacific's northernmost Idaho enterprise, the Spokane International, operates 140 miles of track between Spokane and Eastport on the Canadian border. At first glance the SI may seem nothing more than a branch line, but it is actually part of a Soo Line–CP Rail–UP transcontinental route that extends from Spokane to the Midwest via Canada.

Iowa-born Daniel Chase Corbin (who had built railroads into Nelson, B.C., and Wallace, Idaho) constructed the Spokane International with Canadian Pacific Railway money in 1905–1906. It was Canadian Pacific's way of taking business away from the Great Northern, which was hard at work extending rail lines into the mining regions of southern British Columbia at CPR's expense.

The Spokane International met the Canadian Pacific-owned British Columbia Southern Railway at Curzon, B.C. (near Yahk), on November 1, 1906. Twin Cities–Spokane passenger service was inaugurated the follow-

ing summer on the newly created transcontinental route, which was 55 miles longer than the Great Northern, but 14 miles shorter than the Northern Pacific. At one time the route was competitive enough to steal a U.S. Mail contract away from rival Great Northern.

Canadian Pacific purchased the Spokane International outright in 1916, but during the Depression the SI fell into bankruptcy. CPR held on to the Yahk–Kingsgate (B.C.) portion of the line, and in 1941 the Spokane International was reorganized as an independent carrier. Union Pacific purchased the line on January 1, 1959, and in 1987 the Spokane International corporate identity was eliminated altogether.

Service to Spokane, Eastport and Coeur d'Alene keeps the Spokane International busy today. Despite a rather checkered history, it appears that Mr. Corbin's last effort at railroad building has succeeded after all.

(Right): CP Rail northbound train No. 9 prepares to leave Eastport for Cranbrook, B.C. Its southbound UP counterpart this August 21, 1988 morning, the CPHK (Canadian Pacific-Hinkle), did not leave until later that afternoon.

(Above): SI's Sandpoint–Moyie Springs Local creaks across the ancient Kootenai River bridge at Bonners Ferry on September 11, 1978. The wooden Howe truss bridge—last of its kind to be used in the Northwest—collapsed under the weight of a train in December 1985. It has since been replaced with a steel and concrete structure (see page 89). (Left): Earlier that day, the Moyie Local was in the hole at Samuels to meet train No. 9, powered by CP Rail SD40-2s. UP–CPR motive power pools were established in the mid-1970s and have continued sporadically ever since.

KOOTENAI CANYON VIEWS

The 900-foot descent from Eastport to Bonners Ferry may appear dramatic in places, but in fact represents a grade of only 0.5 percent. (Above): UP's CPHK—90 cars strong—crosses a trestle high above the Kootenai River (and the BN main line) two miles west of Moyie Springs on August 21, 1988. (Right): Another long train whines downhill a mile further west on August 5, 1983. The speed limit along this stretch: 15 mph.

The Wallace Branches

THOUGH THE Union Pacific–Northern Pacific interchange at Wallace resulted in an additional route across Idaho, the sum of the two was never meant to serve as a main line. The two branches were content enough serving Idaho's booming Coeur d'Alene mining district, which to date has produced over $4 billion worth of gold, silver, lead and zinc.

Gold was first discovered along the North Fork at the Coeur d'Alene River in 1882, triggering a gold rush that lasted two years. The legendary Bunker Hill claim was made in 1885 by which time lead and silver were being mined as well.

The Mullan Road (built in 1860–1863) proved inadequate to transport the heavy ores, and two railroads, the Coeur d'Alene Railway and Navigation Company and the Washington and Idaho Railroad, were soon incorporated to alleviate the problem. Daniel C. Corbin completed his narrow-gauge CR&N between Mission Landing on Coeur d'Alene Lake and Wallace in 1887. NP acquired a lease on the property in 1888, extending it to Mullan a year later.

The standard-gauge Washington and Idaho Railroad, built by UP's Oregon Railway and Navigation, reached Wallace in 1889 via a branch from OR&N's Spokane main line at Tekoa. Surveys east to Missoula were also completed (including a 6,800-foot-long tunnel under Lookout Pass) with the intent of connecting to UP's Utah and Northern rails in Garrison and J.J. Hill's Montana Central in Butte. W&I rails were extended to Mullan in 1809 at which time work was begun on the tunnel.

To forestall OR&N's intrusion into Montana, NP decided to build a line on the OR&N survey from DeSmet, near Missoula, to Wallace in 1889. Plans to tunnel under Lookout Pass were also considered but to save time, a line burdened with four-percent grades, 16-degree curves and a single switchback was built instead. NP's Coeur d'Alene Branch (later known as the Wallace Branch) was completed to Mullan in late 1890 and CR&N tracks between Mullan and Wallace were standard gauged the following year. Thus defeated, OR&N ceased work on its tunnel. NP never built its tunnel either, though the switchback at Carbonite was later replaced with a horseshoe curve and trestle. (The trestle was torn down and the switchback reopened in 1963.)

UP abandoned its Wallace–Mullan trackage in 1894 as did the NP–CR&N narrow gauge between Mission Landing and Wallace in 1896, thereby eliminating all duplicate trackage. For the next 84 years, rail service in the region consisted of NP's branch from Missoula, UP's branch from Tekoa (later, Plummer Junction) and several UP/NP spurs.

The expense of maintaining 57 miles of mountainous trackage (includ-ing 19 miles of leased Milwaukee Road right-of-way) eventually forced BN to abandon its Wallace Branch. BN's last train left Wallace on September 2, 1980, and within a year, rails that had been in place for 90 years were removed.

Today, only one train—UP's Kellogg Local from Spokane—calls on the Coeur d'Alene mining district, where such enterprises as the Sunshine, Bunker Hill and Lucky Friday mines found riches in the hillsides above the rails. Those hills still produce more silver and lead than anywhere else in America and as long as the mines keep working, so too will Wallace Branch trains.

A view of Wallace from Northern Pacific's elegant brick depot, built in 1902. The structure, listed in the National Register of Historic Places, has since been moved to accommodate the construction of Interstate 90.

EASTWARD ALONG BN'S WALLACE BRANCH, JUNE 8, 1979

(Right): Climbing the four-percent grade between Carbonite and Lookout Pass. Moments earlier, the locomotives and caboose exchanged positions on the single switchback at Carbonite. (Above): The head brakeman aligns the turnout onto the Milwaukee Road main line at Haugan, Montana, where BN had trackage rights on the Milwaukee east to St. Regis. Flood damage forced NP to abandon its own line between Haugan and St. Regis in 1933 and for a few months after the March 1980 Milwaukee Road shutdown, BN had this portion of Milwaukee's main line all to itself.

UP'S MILLION-DOLLAR TRAINS

(Above left): Switching the Bunker Hill–Sullivan mines in Kellogg, July 25, 1983. Each of those gondolas carries a load of silver-lead ore worth one million dollars. (Left): When BN abandoned its Wallace Branch in 1980, UP purchased the Wallace–Mullan segment to reach the Lucky Friday Mine. In this 1983 view, the crew on the Kellogg Local has stopped for beans before heading upriver to Mullan.

(Opposite): UP geeps accelerate a short train across the marshlands near Cataldo on July 28, 1983. There are no grades and few curves from here to Lake Coeur d'Alene and the hogger will likely stretch the 35-mph speed limit to an easy 50.

Milwaukee's Unelectrified Gap

MANY RAILROAD divisions have been overshadowed by more famous (or infamous) neighbors over the years. Such is certainly the case with Milwaukee Road's 212 miles of main line wedged between the two well-publicized electrified divisions, and known simply as the "gap."

The last transcontinental to build through the state (in 1908), the Milwaukee entered Idaho via St. Paul Pass and descended 1,700 feet into Avery, division point and western terminus of the 440-mile electrified Rocky Mountain Division. West of Avery, Milwaukee tracks followed the St. Joe River into St. Maries, then climbed along the southern edge of Coeur d'Alene Lake toward Plummer Junction and points west.

The Milwaukee main line bypassed Spokane by 30 miles, so a connection was achieved by building a line north from Plummer Junction to UP's Amwaco Branch at Manito in 1912. To reach Spokane from the west, Milwaukee trains were granted trackage rights on UP's Spokane main line from Marengo. Spokane area freights and all passenger trains used this longer route.

Electrification of the Milwaukee Road main line between Harlowton and Avery was completed in 1916 and on the Coast Division three years later. Electrifying the resulting gap had been considered (Coast Division substation numbers took the possibility into account) but the idea was shelved in 1921. Aging electric equipment and high maintenance costs led to the end of Milwaukee's electric operations in 1974.

The last Milwaukee Road freight left St. Maries on March 17, 1980. A majority of the main line west of Plummer and east of Avery was abandoned, but the Plummer–Avery main line and the Elk River Branch to Bovill were purchased by Potlatch Forests Incorporated, which began operating the St. Maries River Railroad two months later.

Though the Milwaukee Road will be sorely missed, it's both ironic and heartening to note that at least a portion of this "largely uninspiring" gap (to quote one eastern writer) is still alive and well.

Milwaukee train No. 205 slows to pick up orders at Avery on September 10, 1978. This legendary little town was the western terminus of Milwaukee's electrified Rocky Mountain division until 1974; now it is a railroad ghost town.

(Right): Train time at Plummer Junction during the summer of 1978. (Below): Two SD40-2s take a west-bound freight across Pedee Viaduct on September 9, 1978. Two more SD40-2s are positioned midtrain to assist in the one-percent climb to Plummer Junction.

ST. MARIES RIVER RAILROAD

After the Milwaukee Road suspended operations through Idaho in 1980, portions of its right-of-way between Bovill, St. Maries and Plummer remained in service under court-ordered "directed service" to support local logging operations. Potlatch acquired 115 miles of the line and on May 23, 1980, the St. Maries River Railroad (STMA) opened for business.

The STMA is comprised of Milwaukee's Elk River Branch to Bovill (built in 1910) and the Avery–St. Maries–Plummer portion of the Milwaukee Road main line. The St. Maries–Avery segment became a private, non-common carrier called the St. Maries Logging Railroad. Avery operations were the subject of a court battle in which the U.S. Forest Service wanted to reclaim 13 miles of Milwaukee right-of-way between Marble Creek and Avery. The courts decided for the Forest Service, and the Avery Logger made its last run in November 1984.

GP9s and SW1200s continue to carry Potlatch logs and lumber over Milwaukee rails between St. Maries, the Union Pacific in Plummer and BN's Washington, Idaho and Montana Railway in Bovill. The St. Maries River Railroad has thus become part of a small cadre of short lines (including the Washington Central, Central Montana and Pend Oreille Valley) that have found success in the ruins of Milwaukee's failure.

(Below): STMA facilities at St. Maries: the depot and the former Milwaukee geeps have been rebuilt, but the maintenance shop is new. (Left): The Bovill Local climbing St. Maries River Canyon near Santa, July 26, 1983.

THE AVERY LOGGER, July 23, 1983

(Above): STMA's two SW1200s take a string of loaded log cars along the St. Joe River a few miles west of Avery. (Left): Heading up the canyon with empties, east of St. Joe. The tracks through here were removed in 1987.

Camas Prairie RR Co.

THE CAMAS PRAIRIE RAILROAD is a Northwest unique not simply because of its famous bridges or Lapwai Canyon, but because of its joint operating arrangement created by archrivals UP and NP. The Camas Prairie never owned any locomotives, freight cars or right-of-way, but does operate 254 miles of railroad reaching into the timberlands along the Clearwater River and the wheat fields of its namesake prairie.

The town of Lewiston wanted a railroad so desperately that in 1890 it offered a $100,000 subsidy to Northern Pacific's Spokane and Palouse Railroad to build a line into town. The NP agreed and within a month, grading contracts had been awarded. A year later, rails reached Juliaetta, 22 miles north of Lewiston, where construction halted for seven years due to the Panic of 1893. When the first train arrived in Lewiston on September 15, 1898, the townsfolk put on a celebration that lasted three days.

Northern Pacific incorporated the Clearwater Short Line Railway two months later to construct two branches: one east along the Clearwater River and the other south to Grangeville on the Camas Prairie high above the river. It was anticipated that the Clearwater River line might cross Lolo Pass into Missoula creating a shorter NP main line, but surveys indicated that this was too costly. Tracklaying thus stopped at Stites in 1900.

Work on the Grangeville Branch was halted at Culdesac in 1899 when objections from UP's Oregon Railroad & Navigation were raised. UP claimed the line violated an 1880 agreement in which the NP agreed not to build branch lines south of the Snake River (the Grangeville Branch is northeast of the river). The situation appeared resolved in 1901 when NP President C.S. Mellon announced that NP or OR&N would build a line between Lewiston and Riparia (located on OR&N's Spokane main line). Furthermore, a 1905 agreement allowed NP trackage rights over a proposed UP Lewiston–Riparia line in exchange for allowing UP access to Grangeville. Construction on the Grangeville Branch was thus resumed in 1906 and completed two years later.

UP's Riparia–Lewiston line was completed by its subsidiary Oregon, Washington and Idaho Railroad in 1908. The next year, the SP&S constructed a branch from its main line at Snake River Junction to Riparia, which NP purchased in June 1909. The two rivals signed an agreement on November 4, 1909, establishing a jointly owned company named the Camas Prairie Railroad to manage operations between Riparia, Lewiston and Grangeville (but not on the Kamiah Branch to Stites). Locomotives and operating crews were to be supplied equally by the NP and UP, though each would retain ownership of existing rights-of-way, bridges and structures. Camas Prairie retained revenue generated on-line; NP and UP retained revenue earned off-line.

An Orofino–Headquarters branch was built in 1927 as part of an agreement made with the Clearwater Timber Company (a Potlatch predecessor) to haul logs to a new sawmill in Lewiston. The Camas Prairie agreement was amended the following year to include this branch as well as the Kamiah Branch to Stites.

Cutbacks in recent years have changed Camas Prairie operations somewhat. Dams completed on the Snake River in the 1960s and 1970s gave the Camas Prairie a new Lewiston–Riparia right-of-way, but they also provided large-scale grain barge access to Lewiston. Unable to compete with barge shipping rates, Camas Prairie grain traffic dropped precipitously. BN's "Highball" freights from Lewiston to Spokane over the Arrow Line made their last trips in 1983 (traffic is now routed via Riparia to Pasco). The last 10 miles of the Headquarters Branch were abandoned the same year and in 1984, 1.7 miles of track west of Stites were taken out of service. Even the Lewiston depot has been sold.

UP and NP cabooses (both in outdated lettering schemes) share tracks at East Lewiston on July 27, 1983.

Business on the Headquarters and Kamiah Branches appears secure, but such is not the case on the Grangeville Branch. Its business decimated by the river barges and a dwindling number of active sawmills, BN has made no secret of its intention to abandon this most famous of all Idaho branch lines.

If and when the Grangeville Branch is abandoned, the railroad world will never be quite the same. For the present, however, the spectacle of squealing flanges, brake smoke and roaring geeps in Lapwai Canyon—the essence of Camas Prairie railroading—will continue a little while longer.

(Right): UP and BN geeps throttle up a notch as they pull the Grangeville Local across Lawyers Canyon Bridge, largest and most imposing on the railroad, on September 8, 1978. (Below): Camas Prairie train No. 886, the "Night Logger" to Orofino, crosses the Clearwater River near Spalding on July 27, 1983. When times are good, No. 886 handles as many as 200 cars.

HEADQUARTERS BRANCH

(Above left): A caboose hop traverses Reeds Creek in 1983, the last year of operation over the 3,521-foot summit to Headquarters. The lead unit, Camas Prairie veteran No. 1702, got a new nose after it derailed and landed in the Clearwater River in 1975. (Above): Four geeps lift a long string of logs up the 2.2-percent grade above Headquarters on August 24, 1977. (Left): A Jeep hyrail pauses at the Orofino depot while geeps of another kind await their daily assignment to Headquarters.

KAMIAH BRANCH

(Above): A short Kamiah Local steps carefully over the old Clearwater River bridge at Kamiah on July 26, 1983. The non-operating swing span was scheduled for replacement years earlier, but still carries trains today, just as it has since it was installed—secondhand—in 1899. (Right): End of track at Stites, where NP surveyors once had their sights set on Lolo Pass and Missoula.

GRANGEVILLE BRANCH

The Grangeville Branch is Camas Prairie's most famous due in no small part to Lapwai Canyon, whose 3,000-foot ascent onto the prairielands is considered by many to be one of the seven wonders of the railroad world. The 14 miles of three-percent grade between Culdesac and Reubens alone required 17 bridges and seven tunnels that took nearly three years and $4 million to complete.

(Left): A 21-car train climbs Lapwai Canyon near Nucrag on a rainy September 8, 1978. After circumnavigating a horseshoe curve, the train will reappear on the trestles in the background. (Above): The following morning, the Grangeville Local approaches the "main line" (1st Subdivision) at Spalding. The milepost on the left indicates there are 126.2 miles to Marshall via NP's Spokane and Palouse Branch (abandoned south of Moscow in 1983).

(Below): On August 24, 1977, the Grangeville Local crosses one of the branch's 45 trestles (2½ miles' worth), this one near Cottonwood. (Right): The Grangeville Local a year later near Ferdinand. There's only one grain car on this train; the rest is lumber and wood chips.

NEZPERCE RAILROAD

When it was discovered that Nezperce would be bypassed by NP's Grangeville Branch, Zephaniah Johnson raised $211,000 from townsfolk to build a line from Nezperce to Lewiston. The result was the 13.4-mile Nezperce and Idaho Railroad, which reached Camas Prairie rails at Craigmont in 1910.

Ownership of the N&I changed hands several times over the years and in 1944, local farmer John J. Lux bought the property for $25,000, renaming it the Nezperce Railroad. The right-of-way had deteriorated badly over the years. Trips sometimes took days to complete and on one such adventure, there were 13 derailments. The track was eventually rebuilt and in 1950, a pair of used Plymouth diesels replaced the 1901-vintage steam locomotive (a 2-6-2 *Prairie*, naturally).

The Nezperce led a quiet existence until the late 1970s, when demands by customers for heavier 100-ton grain hoppers (which wouldn't run on the line's 56-pound rails) and Snake River barge competition delivered fatal blows. Trucks took over the business, and at times, Nezperce trains didn't run for months. The line was embargoed in 1981 and for nearly two years its right-of-way was used to store idle Railbox cars. Under pressure from the ICC to resume service, the Nezperce filed for abandonment in 1983. The last revenue run was made that spring; rails have since been removed from the prairies that Nezperce trains roamed for over 70 years.

(Below): Orange GE 45-tonner No. 7115, one of three purchased from the Air Force in 1971. (Below left): The local to Craigmont awaits departure from Nezperce in 1978. In later years the railroad had no full-time employees; crews took time off regular jobs to run the trains.

A PRAIRIE PASTORAL

(Above): A seven-car Nezperce freight heads for Craigmont at a leisurely 10 mph on September 8, 1978. (Right): A half hour later, the train lurches into Craigmont, fighting wobbly rail, weeds and a three-percent grade.

Western Montana

MONTANA. Its very name means mountain, and there are plenty of mountains here. But in spite of the Big Belt, Bitterroot and Bridger mountains encountered en route, railroad builders managed to construct three transcontinental lines across the state as well as far-reaching branches of the Union Pacific, Soo Line and Burlington. Their ingenuity once allowed us to cross Marias Pass in the comfort of Great Northern Great Domes, climb Sixteen Mile canyon behind Milwaukee Road Little Joe electrics and follow the trail of Lewis and Clark on board Northern Pacific's *North Coast Limited.*

No other region of the Northwest has experienced more recent changes in rail transportation than Montana. First came the BN merger and Amtrak in 1970 and 1971, followed by the collapse of Milwaukee Road in 1980. The Butte, Anaconda and Pacific was sold in 1985 and sizable portions of the former NP main line are now operated by the Montana Western and Montana Rail Link. Only Soo Line's Whitetail Branch in the northeast corner of the state and Union Pacific's Butte Line remain untouched—so far.

Montana's first railroad was the narrow-gauge Utah and Northern, which arrived from Utah with great fanfare in 1880. UP SD40-2s have long since replaced U&N 2-6-0s, but it still takes two crossings of the Continental Divide to reach Butte. Though hard hit by the collapse of Butte's copper industry, UP traffic has rebounded somewhat with the help of newcomers Montana Western and Rarus Railway, and a modest reopening of the Butte mines.

Northern Pacific arrived from Dakota Territory on its way to Puget Sound in 1882. NP President Henry Villard celebrated the completion of the Northwest's first transcontinental in grand style at Gold Creek, Montana, the following year.

Yet another empire builder, James J. Hill, entered Montana in 1887 by way of the St. Paul, Minneapolis and Manitoba Railway. By 1890, Hill was hard at work building the Great Northern Railway west of Havre and within a few short years, his GN empire would have more route-miles in Montana than any other railroad.

And then there was the Milwaukee Road. A once prosperous granger line, the Chicago, Milwaukee and St. Paul sought to secure a stronghold in the Northwest by extending its rails across Montana to Puget Sound in the early 1900s. After three bankruptcies and decades of red ink, however, "America's Resourceful Railroad" was forced to abandon its Pacific Coast Extension in 1980. In between the promise made and the promise broken were its pioneering use of tricolor block signals, the electrification of 710 miles of main line and innovative Super Dome *Olympian Hiawathas.* To those who had grown fond of this once great enterprise, it was indeed sad to say farewell to the Milwaukee and its Hiawatha spirit.

The coming of the Burlington Northern merger in 1970 brought the obvious casualties: no more Rocky or Big Sky Blue, no more NP monad. In the process, BN inherited a network of GN and NP main lines and branch lines spread across Montana as well as a pair of strategic Burlington lines leading to Colorado and Nebraska.

To suggest that BN dominates Montana railroading today would be an understatement, but that domination has recently been reduced somewhat with the leasing of NP's former Sandpoint–Huntley main line to Montana Rail Link in 1987. Such action reflects a somewhat controversial BN corporate policy of shedding redundant mileage and the desire to operate trains with two-man crews, which in the case of the MRL has led to court battles, a wildcat strike and equipment sabotage.

Montana has been through some tough times, but it's still a land of great promise. Certainly those early railroad builders felt that way, too.

BN's Wallace Branch Local rolls into Montana at Lookout Pass on June 8, 1979. This historic line was abandoned in 1980.

A ray of sunlight embraces a westward Amtrak *Empire Builder* approaching Glacier
Park and the Montana Rockies on June 24, 1973.

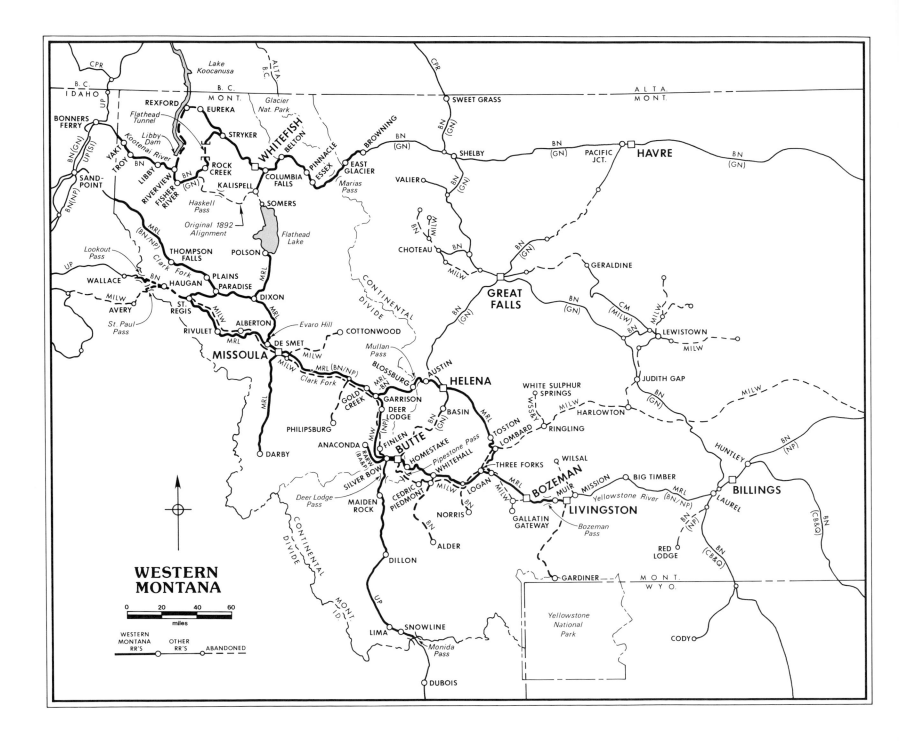

WESTERN MONTANA

Big Sky Railroading, clockwise from above: A 1979-vintage *Empire Builder* passes F9 helpers at Essex; a Milwaukee Road–Butte, Anaconda and Pacific triple meet at Rocker, June 3, 1979; UP train No. 289 in the Big Hole River Canyon at Maiden Rock, June 23, 1987; a Milwaukee Road freight at Donald siding on the Continental Divide, August 28, 1975.

BN's High Line

A FEW YEARS AGO, nostalgic "Rocky Lives" stencils began appearing on the flanks of former GN locomotives, in fond remembrance of Great Northern's mountain goat mascot who first appeared in 1921. Though now retired, Rocky still evokes visions of bright red cabooses, sleek *Empire Builders* and the Rocky Mountain region through which they traveled.

"Rocky Lives" stencils on F45 No. 6625 at Seattle, April 20, 1985.

James J. Hill's Great Northern Railway began building westward from Pacific Junction (near Havre) in 1890. GN pathfinders John F. Stevens and Charles F.B. Haskell initially considered two possible routes. One would use Hill's existing Montana Central line to Helena, then head west to Spokane paralleling the Northern Pacific. The other route headed west along the Canadian border, crossing the Continental Divide at a point known only to local natives and trappers. Stevens located the crossing, known today as Marias Pass (dedicated to Captain Meriwether Lewis' cousin, Maria Wood), on December 11, 1889. Haskell explored the Flathead River country west of the Divide the following spring, locating a route through the Cabinet Range into the Kootenai River watershed and Idaho.

Track construction over Marias Pass was accomplished from both sides in 1891. By 1893, GN tracklayers had reached Scenic in the Cascade Mountains east of Seattle, where GN's last spike was driven on January 6th.

During the 80-year span of GN's residence in Montana, no less than three successive routes were utilized between the Flathead and Kootenai River watersheds. The original 1892 route crossed Haskell Pass west of Kalispell. The second route took advantage of GN's Montana and Great Northern Railway, which built north from the GN main line at Jennings to the Elk River Valley of British Columbia in 1901–1902. Construction of a connecting line from Columbia Falls to the M&GN at Rexford in 1903–1904 resulted in a new main line that was 16 miles longer, but with ruling grades (0.7 percent) that were half that of the Haskell Pass line.

Construction of the Libby Dam in the 1960s required yet another line relocation. Sixty miles of new railroad was constructed over the Cabinet Range between Jennings (now Riverview) and Stryker, including the 6.69-mile-long Flathead Tunnel, the seventh longest tunnel in the world at the time. The Libby Bypass opened on November 7, 1970.

Under BN management, traffic on the "High Line" (as it was known after the merger) increased substantially when Northern Pacific's main line through Missoula was relegated to secondary status. Additional traffic increases were anticipated when Montana Rail Link went into service in 1987 (thereby diverting some of the NP business over the High Line and the former GN Great Falls–Billings line). BN is exercising its run-through rights on the MRL, however, and traffic patterns have remained about the same.

SD60s, Superliners and Twin-Stacks are the current order of the day along BN's High Line, but there is still much of the old Great Northern evident in the depots, along the right-of-way and in the high country that GN adopted as its corporate image—the land where Rocky lives.

(Above): A more traditional portrait of Rocky on a vermilion red GN boxcar owned by the Lake Whatcom Railway in Wickersham, Washington. (Above right): A Glacier Park Company limousine meets the morning *Empire Builder* at Belton in 1983, a summer tradition as old as the park itself. (Right): BN's No. 104 crossing Tunnel Creek in Flathead River country near Pinnacle, March 17, 1986.

KOOTENAI COUNTRY

(Left): On March 22, 1987, an eastbound freight works its way up Kootenai River Canyon near Yakt, lowest point in Montana (1,800 feet). (Above): GE 45-tonner No. 7 switches the St. Regis Paper Mill at Libby in August 1983. (Below): Rustic decor in the waiting room at Libby.

THE LIBBY BYPASS

Completed in 1970, the 60-mile Libby Bypass is a superb example of modern railway engineering, characterized by sweeping curves, massive fills and Flathead Tunnel. Ironically, the new right-of-way between Riverview and Tamarack follows the original 1892 Haskell Pass alignment, abandoned in 1905.

(Right): Train No. 103 heads downgrade near Rock Creek with parts of a Boeing 737 in tow on March 22, 1987. (Above right): Amtrak's *Empire Builder* emerges from the east portal of Flathead Tunnel at 5:33 a.m., June 3, 1979. To the left of the train are twin 2,000-hp tunnel ventilation fans capable of moving a third of a million cubic feet per minute.

WHITEFISH AT SUNRISE

Whitefish has been a busy division point since GN's Columbia Falls–Rexford cutoff was completed in 1904. (The actual division point is 10.5 miles further east at Conkelley, where double-track territory ends.) Besides having a modest freight yard and a large frame depot, Whitefish is also home to one of Montana's last roundhouses.

(Above left): Power for the Cut Bank Local watches hotshot train No. 1 get a quick change of crews on St. Patrick's Day morning, 1986. (Left): Right on the advertised—6:35 a.m.—Amtrak's eastbound *Empire Builder* eases to a stop in front of the Whitefish depot on August 3, 1983.

IZAAK WALTON, ESSEX AND BELTON CANYON

Located at the foot of the 18-mile Walton Hill, Essex was established as a helper station soon after GN rails arrived in 1891. During the glory days of steam, Essex was home to 400 people, three water tanks and a coal dock.

(Above): F9 helpers are added to Train 2-84 on June 3, 1979, for the push up Walton Hill, continuing a tradition that began with FTs in 1941. (Below): The Izaak Walton Inn (named for the 17th-century British naturalist) was built for helper crews in 1939 and is now a favorite of railfans. (Right): In Belton Canyon west of Essex, No. 103 heads follows the Flathead River toward Whitefish on March 17, 1986.

ACROSS THE DIVIDE

(Left): Train No. 88 roars up the 1.8-percent grade west of Marias on June 4, 1979, with an F45-F45-U33C combination leading and a quartet of F9s pushing. The Whitefish-based F9s made their last push on July 20, 1980. (Below): With the helpers removed, No. 88 crests Marias Pass at Summit, lowest crossing (5,213 feet) of the Rocky Mountains in the continental U.S.

Safely over the Divide, train No. 90 crosses Two Medicine bridge—GN's highest—on June 4, 1979. The train is headed for Spotted Robe, Kremlin and eventually, St. Paul.

Union Pacific Country

ON MARCH 9, 1880, a "first spike" ceremony took place atop Monida Pass on the Idaho–Montana border. As the spike was driven home, crowds cheered as far away as Butte, for Montana finally had a railroad, the narrow-gauge Utah and Northern. When completed in 1882, the 454-mile U&N became one of the largest narrow-gauge enterprises in America, forming the northern extremity of a continuous network of slim rails that reached all the way to Santa Fe, New Mexico.

Montana's mining boom led to the building of a wagon road in the 1860s, extending south to the Union Pacific railhead at Corinne, Utah. Mormon Church leaders saw promise in building a competing rail line and on August 23, 1871, the Utah Northern Railroad Company was incorporated.

The Panic of 1873 forced the suspension of tracklaying soon after Utah Northern rails reached the Idaho border in 1874. Union Pacific purchased the line in 1878, and construction of the reorganized Utah and Northern Railway Company resumed shortly thereafter.

The U&N reached Butte in 1881 and Garrison the following year in anticipation of meeting the Northern Pacific tracks advancing westward from Helena. (Dual-gauge trackage rights over the NP to Helena were discussed, but never granted.)

After UP's Oregon Short Line was completed across Idaho in 1884, most U&N tonnage ended up being transloaded to and from standard-gauge cars at Pocatello. The Silver Bow–Garrison segment was standard gauged after it was leased to the UP–NP jointly owned Montana Union Railroad in 1886, and it was therefore decided to widen the balance of the narrow-gauge tracks north of Pocatello to eliminate the costly transloading process. Trackage was gradually rebuilt with standard-gauge ties and heavier rail (though still at narrow gauge) and on July 24, 1887, an army of 400 workers regauged the entire 255-mile line in a single day.

UP's standard-gauged "Butte Line" prospered as Thomas Edison's electric inventions and World War I caused dramatic increases in Butte's copper production. Helper terminals were established at Dubois and Lima to service the 2-8-8-0s and 4-6-6-4s brought north to handle the additional traffic. The line continued its profitable existence as a mainline carrier of copper, agricultural products and passengers (the latter via the *Butte Special)* until only recently.

UP's Silver Bow/Butte business may have suffered somewhat when the Milwaukee Road suspended Pacific Extension operations in 1980, but the subsequent closure of Butte's copper mining operations was devastating. Copper mining in Butte has since resumed on a modest scale, and interchange business with newcomers Rarus Railway and Montana Western has improved accordingly. Increasing expenses, however, forced the UP to put the Butte Line up for sale in 1986. Though both the Montana Western and Montana Rail Link have expressed an interest, the line remains unsold.

For the present, UP trains continue their century-long passage through this unforgiving land, battling the snows and grades of its narrow-gauge heritage, in the shadows of an uncertain future.

The caboose of a northbound freight rolls by the Dillon depot on August 1, 1983. Though only 69 rail miles south of Butte, Dillon is UP's only crew change point in Montana.

SILVER BOW

(Above): An interesting GP30-DD35B-GP9B-SD40 power combination pauses alongside BN's Silver Bow depot before proceeding into Butte on August 4, 1974. (Right): Switching Silver Bow yard took no time at all during the dark times of the early 1980s. The train this August 1, 1983 morning left town with only eight cars.

(Above): UP's Montana rails never venture far from magnificent mountain vistas and this June 6, 1979 view of train No. 278 near Snowline is no exception. (Right): A half hour later, No. 278 has reached the Continental Divide at Monida, highest existing railroad pass (6,870 feet) in Montana.

(Opposite): A quartet of SD40-2s crosses the Continental Divide at Deer Lodge Pass with 38 loads, 11 empties and a C&NW caboose on June 23, 1987. 5,902-foot Deer Lodge Pass had been the intended route of the Northern Pacific before the Utah and Northern built through here in 1881.

The Yellowstone Park Line

ACROSS MONTANA, from Custer to Big Timber to Paradise, lies a century-old, 800-mile steel trail once known as the Northern Pacific Railway. General William Tecumseh Sherman once said, "The West can never be settled, nor protected, without the railroad." Such was certainly the case in Montana in the late 1800s, for the contribution that the "Yellowstone Park Line" made in its development is clearly evident: every major city in the state (except Great Falls) is located along the NP main line.

The Northern Pacific Railroad Company was chartered in Congress on July 2, 1864, to extend from Lake Superior to Puget Sound. Groundbreaking ceremonies near Duluth didn't take place until 1870 and NP's bankruptcy following the Panic of 1873 forced construction to halt at Bismarck, N.D. A reorganized NP was on its way again in 1879 under the direction of Frederick Billings, pushing west from Bismarck and east from Wallula, Washington.

In Montana, NP's track gangs followed the Yellowstone River for 340 miles, then climbed over Bozeman Pass. The original 1869 survey called for crossing the Continental Divide at Deer Lodge Pass near Butte, but

NP Chief Engineer Adna Anderson decided on a Mullan Pass route—40 miles shorter, but requiring the construction of a 3,800-foot-long tunnel across the summit.

NP rails from the east and west met at Gold Creek, near Garrison, on August 22, 1883. NP President Henry Villard (who had acquired control of the NP in 1881) arranged for one of the most elaborate last spike ceremonies in American history. Five special trains brought dignitaries (including U.S. Grant, Joseph Pulitzer and George M. Pullman) to the site and at 5:18 p.m., September 8, 1883, a crowd of 3,000 celebrated the completion of a dream that began 19 years earlier.

The cost of completing that dream, however, had been staggering. Construction costs far exceeded estimates and Villard was forced to tap lines of credit from NP's parent company, the Oregon and Transcontinental (which also controlled the OR&N and the Oregon and California Railroad). NP stock prices dropped badly after this revelation, and Villard's financial empire soon collapsed. Four months after NP's last spike was driven, Villard was forced to resign his post as NP president.

In the ensuing years, NP built an extensive network of branch lines in Montana as well as alternate main lines via Butte and St. Regis. Great Northern's J.J. Hill secured control of the NP after the Panic of 1893 and for decades thereafter, Hill interests sought to merge the two lines. When the Burlington Northern merger took place in 1970, NP's Montana main line became secondary to GN's High Line (though it continues to be used for Pacific Coast–Midwest–Gulf Coast traffic).

Montana Rail Link's 1987 lease of former NP trackage between Sandpoint, Idaho, and Huntley (near Billings) was intended to operate through-BN trains and provide local service with longer crew districts and fewer crews; its debut was anything but uneventful. Within hours of MRL's Halloween morning startup, three locomotives were uncoupled from a train in Livingston and allowed to run unattended over Bozeman Pass, overturning just past the summit. The United Transportation Union staged a wildcat strike throughout Montana that morning, halted a few hours later by a U.S. District Court injunction.

Such is progress. From Northern Pacific to Burlington Northern and now, Montana Rail Link. Will this latest heir to the Yellowstone Park Line prove a worthy successor? Only time will tell.

Northern Pacific S-4 class 4-6-0 (Baldwin, 1902) on display in Missoula.
Number 1356 was retired in 1954 after logging more than a million miles during her half-century tenure on the "Yellowstone Park Line."

(Above): On July 28, 1983, former NP geeps bring the Paradise Local into Paradise, junction of the 3rd Subdivision Evaro Hill main (right) and the 5th Subdivision St. Regis main (foreground). (Right): Extra 6833 West glides along the banks of the Clark Fork near Plains (originally "Horse Plains") on March 16, 1986.

(Above right): The monad, ancient symbol of the Orient, was adopted by the NP after its chief engineer, E.H. McHenry, saw a Korean flag at the 1893 Chicago World's Fair. By 1900, NP was using the symbol everywhere, including the Livingston station where this example was found.

ALONG THE ST. REGIS MAIN LINE

The Missoula–St. Regis portion of NP's Coeur d'Alene (Wallace) Branch was transformed into an alternate main line when the 22-mile St. Regis–Paradise cutoff was completed in 1909. Though 28 miles longer than the original main line over Evaro Hill, the St. Regis main followed the course of the Clark Fork, thereby avoiding grades—and helper districts. (BN took the Evaro Hill main out of service in 1983.)

(Left): BN No. 104 roars across Fish Creek trestle east of Rivulet on June 22, 1987.
(Above): Colorado and Southern SD40-2 No. 912 and a U25C duck under the Milwaukee Road main line at St. Regis with train No. 85 on June 10, 1979.

MISSOULA LOCALS

During the BN years, Missoula-based crews operated locals to Darby and Polson (via Paradise). (Right): The Monday-only Darby Local of June 15, 1987, leaves Missoula along the Bitter Root Branch, which began life as the Missoula and Bitter Root Valley Railroad in 1887. (Below right): Heading back to Missoula, the Polson Local climbs above Flathead Lake on June 24, 1987. The Polson Branch was completed in 1918.

THE CLIMB FROM HELENA

(Left): NP's 1864 charter limited grades to 196 feet per mile (2.2 percent), so surveyors were forced to lay a giant double loop of track near Austin to reach Mullan Pass legally. In this view, "double grain" train GM5MC coils around the upper loop on June 17, 1987, helpers visible in the background.

(Below left): In Helena (originally called "Last Chance Gulch"), NP's colonial-style station once hosted the *Alaskan* and *Mainstreeter* secondary trains, but NP's flagship *North Coast Limited* and Amtrak preferred Butte. (Below): SD40-2 helpers emerge from the east portal of Mullan Tunnel, fitted in later years with unusual squirrel cage ventilation blowers.

THE BUTTE LINE

NP's 121.9-mile alternate main line between Garrison and Logan was created in 1890 when a connection between Logan and the Montana Union Railroad at Butte was completed. Though the Butte Line was slightly shorter than the Helena Line (by 2.8 miles), the 20-mile, 2.2-percent climb over 6,345-foot Homestake Pass was NP's most strenuous and as such, never heavily used as a through route. The Butte–Whitehall segment has not been used since 1982.

(Above): After a short trip up the Butte Line to Three Forks, the Helena–Livingston Local holds for eastbound No. 120 at Logan, junction of the Butte and Helena main lines, on June 16, 1987. Scenes like this are now rare; Montana's mandatory caboose law was declared unconstitutional later that year. (Left): Further west, Amtrak's *North Coast Hiawatha* passes through Jefferson Canyon on August 3, 1974.

BN train No. 271 leaves Livingston for the 13-mile climb to Bozeman Pass on June 20, 1987.

LIVINGSTON

Livingston seems an unlikely place to find heavy locomotive shops, but it was NP's largest diesel servicing facility and in earlier years, one of the few facilities capable of maintaining the road's Z-class Challengers and Yellowstones. BN closed the complex in 1986.

(Above): Former GN observation "Appekunny Mountain" brings up the rear of a 1974-era *North Coast Hiawatha* departing Livingston's 1902-era station. (Right): Livingston Shops as viewed from the transfer table pit. By 1987, this would all belong to Montana Rail Link.

Milwaukee Road's Pacific Coast Extension

THE CHICAGO, Milwaukee and St. Paul Railway was already a well-established granger line when it announced plans to build its 1,400-mile Pacific Coast Extension in 1905. The railroad saw promise in a line of its own to the coast, but 75 years and three bankruptcies later, the Milwaukee Road gave up its quarter billion dollar investment, the largest mainline abandonment in American history.

Construction between Glenham, S.D., and Tacoma began in April 1906 and took three years to complete. Though the easiest passages had long since been occupied by rivals Northern Pacific and Great Northern, Milwaukee bought the Montana Railroad which crossed the Belt Mountains west of Harlowton, then proceeded westward on its own over Pipestone Pass to Butte. Milwaukee then paralleled the Northern Pacific 214 miles to Haugan, where the climb over the Bitterroots and St. Paul Pass began. Crews had already been at work on the Coast and Idaho Divisions and the last spike was driven four miles west of Garrison on May 14, 1909. Construction costs for the Pacific Coast Extension cost nearly four times the $60 million budgeted.

Though not part of the initial construction, electrification had been an integral part of the Pacific Coast Extension design. The decision to electrify the Harlowton–Deer Lodge portion of the main line (with a possible extension to Avery, Idaho) came in 1914 at the urging of John D. Ryan, Milwaukee Road director, president of Anaconda Copper and a major shareholder in several Montana power companies—not exactly a disinterested party.

The $15 million, 440-mile Rocky Mountain Division electrification project—the largest of its kind in the world—was completed in 1916. Running times for electrified trains were reduced as much as 40 percent due to regenerative braking and the inherent smoothness of electric traction. Railroad officials from all over the world came to see Milwaukee's showcase operation, and in later years, so did railfans.

The 1950 purchase of 12 General Electric "Little Joes" kept electrification alive longer than anyone anticipated, but an aging physical plant and a lack of funds to maintain it brought an end to 59 years of electric operations in June 1974.

Few 20th century-built western railroads have ever fared well financially (Canadian National and Western Pacific certainly haven't) and the Milwaukee was no exception. The line fell into receivership in 1925 and again in 1935, managing only three profitable years between 1921 and 1940.

It was thus no surprise when Milwaukee filed for a third reorganization on December 19, 1977. For years, tonnage had often been given away to competitors because too many locomotives were in need of repairs. Track maintenance also suffered, resulting in ever-increasing running times—and derailments.

On November 1, 1979, Milwaukee lines west of Miles City were embargoed. The ICC ordered its reopening for a time, but on February 25, 1980, federal judge Thomas McMillen ordered the shutdown of the Milwaukee Road west of Miles City by the end of the month.

Those final days were not kind to the Milwaukee. The last eastbound revenue freight derailed twice en route and on March 15th, the last train to operate on the Pacific Coast Extension, a motley collection of maintenance equipment left Tacoma—and the Northwest—for good.

Though Milwaukee's Pacific Coast Extension was a failure, its ambitious mainline electrification project, superbly engineered right-of-way and unique "Milwaukee way" of doing things suggest otherwise. Removal of Milwaukee's right-of-way has been heartrending to be sure, but enduring visions of Little Joes, *Olympian Hiawathas* and long freights rolling across the Montana landscape help keep the memories of this once great empire alive.

Triple-headed SD40-2s pull tonnage up the two-percent grade near Cedric on August 29, 1975.

(Above): Little Joes pose at Deer Lodge two months after electric operations ended. Were it not for the Cold War embargo of strategic goods sales to Russia, these GE-built motors (named after Joseph Stalin) would have spent their lives on the Trans-Siberian Railway. (Right): Once the electrics were sidetracked, SD40-2s took over en masse, as evidenced here at Three Forks on August 28, 1975.

(Above left): A short eastbound freight accelerates out of Butte on August 30, 1975. Ahead lie 10 miles of 1.66-percent grade to Pipestone Pass and the Continental Divide. (Left): At Piedmont, the Milwaukee main line began its 21-mile, two-percent eastern ascent of 6,350-foot Pipestone Pass, highest point on the Milwaukee Road. Locotrol-equipped SD40-2s on this 1975 westbound train (identified by their two-digit road numbers) replaced the venerable Butte helper boxcab electrics, which began earning their keep during World War I.

(Above): SD40-2 helpers enter St. Paul Pass tunnel on the Montana–Idaho border in 1979, the last full year of Milwaukee operations to the coast. Ties inside the 8,770-foot tunnel were made of oak. (Right): One of Milwaukee's more whimsical inventions were its wind-powered electric generators mounted atop some cabooses, one of which is seen here at Finlen in 1975. (Above right): After abandonment of the Pacific Coast Extension in 1980, portions of Milwaukee's Montana right-of-way were sold to the L.B. Foster Company of Pittsburgh, which warehoused the track hardware in place until sold. In this view at Haskell siding near Garrison, the discontinuity of rails is all too sobering.

Beautiful Butte

'U GLY AS SIN and just as fascinating" is how historian Stewart Holbrook once described Butte. J. Edgar Hoover used to assign FBI agents there as punishment. Yet for 50 years, Butte and its copper were Montana's largest city and largest industry. It was an enterprise so immense that five railroads found their way into town, the most anywhere in Montana and second only to Spokane and Portland in the entire Northwest.

Gold was discovered in Silver Bow Creek in the 1860s and the collection of tents nearby soon became known as Butte City, named for the peak dominating the town's northern horizon. Silver mining soon overtook placer gold, but silver required stamping mills for processing—and a source of money to build them.

One such source was Marcus Daly, who arrived in the 1870s as an agent for the Walker Brothers of Salt Lake City. After purchasing the Alice Mine for his clients, Daly received an offer to buy an adjacent property in which he discovered a massive vein of copper (of no apparent value to its current owner). Daly bought the mine—called the Anaconda—for himself and with the financial assistance of George Hearst (father of newspaper baron William Randolph Hearst), incorporated the Anaconda Copper Mining Company in 1883.

Butte didn't have enough water to support large-scale copper processing so in 1884, a smelter and company town named Anaconda were completed alongside the Warm Springs River, 26 miles northwest of Butte.

Eventually, "The Big Snake" acquired or merged with all Butte's copper mines and in 1977, Anaconda was purchased by ARCO Petroleum. Plunging copper prices and federal demands to install pollution controls forced the closure of the Anaconda smelter in 1980, and Butte's copper mines three years later.

The fortunes of Butte's five railroads didn't fare much better. The former GN line over Elk Park Pass was the first to be abandoned (in 1972), followed by the entire Milwaukee Road in 1980. BN's Homestake Pass line east of Butte saw its last train in 1982, and the Butte Anaconda and Pacific ceased all but occasional operations when the Butte mines closed. Montana Resources Incorporated (owned by Dennis Washington, who also runs Montana Rail Link) resumed Butte copper mining on a small scale in 1985, allowing newcomer railroads Rarus and Montana Western (and the UP at Silver Bow) to survive on the remains.

Though recent times have not been kind to Butte, geologists claim there's still over a half-billion tons of copper in this "Richest Hill on Earth." Perhaps King Copper will rise again.

The daily Butte, Anaconda and Pacific smelter train leaves town with a string of copper concentrate hoppers on June 5, 1979.

An eastbound Milwaukee Road freight passes through the wye at Pacific Junction (far right) and over the BN main line on June 7, 1979. Butte's namesake peak is in the background.

A CENTURY OF UNION PACIFIC SERVICE

Butte was understandably upset when Garrison was selected as the northern terminus of the narrow-gauge Utah and Northern, but building a seven-mile spur into town involved buying out placer claims that the railroad couldn't afford. Butte citizens rose to the challenge, convincing miners to sell at lower prices and taking up a collection to help purchase them. Thus resolved, Butte's first train arrived on December 26, 1881.

The Butte–Garrison portion of the U&N was standard gauged in 1886 and reorganized as the jointly owned (NP–UP) Montana Union Railroad the same year. Northern Pacific leased the MU for 999 years in 1898 (though UP retained trackage rights into Butte). Traffic declined sharply when copper mining ceased in 1983 and the following year, UP made its last revenue runs into Butte, preferring to terminate its Pocatello trains in nearby Silver Bow.

(Below): A UP train leaves Butte on August 1, 1983, with three carloads of scrap metal, one of the area's main exports these days. The massive Berkeley Pit mine is visible in the background as is Milwaukee Road's station tower (just above the last locomotive).

(Left): Latter-day BN operations in Butte might best be characterized by the fuel hose feeding GP9 No. 1729 draped casually over the main line in front of NP's boarded-up depot. (Below): With only a caboose to keep the couplers taut, BN's Butte Local arrives at Silver Bow to pick up UP interchange traffic, its only source of revenue this August 1983 afternoon.

BUTTE'S GN–NP HERITAGE

Long before the Great Northern was created, the Montana Central Railway reached Butte in 1888 by way of Great Falls and Elk Park Pass. Some speculated that the Montana Central might continue further west, but the transcontinental aspirations of its owner, J.J. Hill, lay further north.

Throughout the years, GN's Butte Division earned its keep hauling copper to a refinery in Great Falls. BN abandoned the Butte–Basin portion of the line in 1972. Since then, the giant Berkeley Pit mine has obliterated much of the old right-of-way, but the roundhouse and station still remain as testament to Rocky's 84-year stay in Butte.

★

Northern Pacific gained access to Butte from Garrison via the Montana Union arrangement of 1886 and on January 14, 1890, a line east over Homestake Pass to Logan was completed, creating an alternate route to the original Helena Line further north.

Because of the steep 2,200-foot climb over Homestake Pass from the east, the Helena main was preferred for most freights. BN freight service into Butte dwindled to a tri-weekly Helena–Garrison–Butte local until 1986, when the Garrison–Butte right-of-way was purchased by the Montana Western.

BUTTE'S OWN—THE BA&P

The Anaconda Copper Company was pleased when the Utah and Northern built a spur line to the new Washoe Smelter at Anaconda in 1884, but under Montana Union ownership a few years later, shipping rates began to rise alarmingly. The Montana Union refused to negotiate, so Anaconda's Marcus Daly built his own railroad, the Butte, Anaconda and Pacific, completed on January 1, 1894.

In 1911, General Electric was awarded a contract to supply the BA&P with 21 electric locomotives, two substations and installation of the 2,400-volt DC catenary, all of which were ready for operation on October 1, 1913. The decision to electrify the line proved to be wise for at its peak, BA&P traffic density reached 30,000 tons per day, requiring almost continuous use of its locomotives on trains as long as 130 cars.

The completion of an ore concentrator in Butte in 1967 reduced BA&P traffic from 12 round trips to one. With six EMD geeps already on the roster and an aging collection of boxcabs, the last electric run was made in April 1968.

Following the closure of the Anaconda smelter in 1980, BA&P trains ran only as required between Butte and Silver Bow (primarily to transport scrap and slag from the smelter). Anaconda filed for abandonment of the BA&P in 1984, but in 1985 the line was purchased by the Rarus Railway. The property was delivered to its new owners in superb condition, a tribute to the pride BA&P displayed throughout its 91-year history of faithful service to King Copper.

(Above): GP7 No. 102 switching empties at Rocker, June 5, 1979. (Below): An early BA&P catenary maintenance vehicle, converted from a World War I-vintage Federal truck, resides today at Butte's Mining Museum.

BA&P's two GP38-2s and a GP9 take the daily smelter train over the BN and Milwaukee main lines in Silver Bow Canyon, June 5, 1979. The GP38s were sold to the Alaska Railroad in 1985.

THE MILWAUKEE WAY

The Milwaukee Road was the last railroad to reach Butte when its track gangs descended into town from Pipestone Pass in 1908. From Pacific Junction west, Milwaukee trains used BA&P tracks through Silver Bow Canyon until its own line was completed six years later.

Milwaukee built a stub-end passenger station on Main Street and maintained a modest yard east of town which veteran Butte helper boxcabs called home for over 50 years.

The last Milwaukee train passed through Butte on March 20, 1980. The only Milwaukee trackage remaining in town today is a small stretch from the former NP–Milwaukee interchange to Newcomb, operated by the Montana Western.

(Left): The Silver Bow Turn, replete with transfer caboose (fifth car back), trundles through Alloy siding on the way to Rocker, June 7, 1979. (Below): A pair of daily trains was all that Milwaukee could muster by 1979, both of which are seen here at Ramsay on June 7th waiting for a BA&P train to pass.

VANISHING VARNISH

In their heyday, Butte's five railroads operated passenger trains from four separate stations (three of them stub-end). The first to appear were Utah and Northern narrow-gauge trains in 1881, followed by BA&P locals and in 1900, NP's legendary *North Coast Limited*.

Milwaukee Road had the distinction of bringing Butte its first streamlined train, the 1947 *Olympian Hiawatha*, and domes (in 1953). GN purchased its only RDC for Butte–Great Falls–Billings service in 1956, which was discontinued in 1961.

Olympian Hiawatha service to Tacoma ended in May 1961, though a court-ordered Deer Lodge–Chicago train lasted until April 1964. The *North Coast Limited* and UP's *Butte Special* made their final runs on the eve of Amtrak Day, 1971, but Amtrak reinstated passenger service on BN's Butte Line six weeks later. Amtrak's *North Coast Hiawatha* fell victim to federal budget cuts in October 1979, and Butte joined the ranks of freight-only towns all across America.

(Above): A quartet of Amtrak F7s coasts along Silver Bow Creek with the eastbound *North Coast Hiawatha* near Rocker on June 26, 1973. Lead unit No. 107 was delivered to the NP in February 1950. (Right): A year later, SDP40Fs had taken over, a pair of which is seen here pulling a multicolored *Hiawatha* consist over Homestake Pass on August 3, 1974.

SURVIVORS IN UNFORGIVING TIMES

On May 1, 1985, three former BA&P employees purchased the BA&P property from the Anaconda Company. The Rarus Railway (named after a Butte copper mine) soon began hauling slag and scrap from Anaconda and beginning in 1986, copper concentrate from Butte.

(Below): Rarus inherited seven GP7s and GP9s from the BA&P, all of which remain in BA&P yellow and black regalia. GP7 No. 101 has since been sold to the Stouffer phosphate plant in Silver Bow and renamed "Li'l Buster." (Right): After dropping off a few covered hoppers at Anaconda's two-mile-long slag pile, a Rarus caboose hop heads for the roundhouse on June 19, 1987. The smelter's brick smokestack, seen in the background, is the world's tallest. (Below right): The twice-weekly Rarus train from Anaconda brings a load of ties, slag hoppers and empty concentrate gons into Rocker on June 19, 1987.

Two of the three Rarus Railway owners resigned in 1986 to form the Montana Western Railway, which operates 60 miles of former NP trackage between Garrison and Butte. MWR trains began running on September 15, 1986, and currently interchanges with the BN and MRL in Garrison, the UP in Silver Bow and the Rarus in Butte.

(Above): Which is which? Rarus GP7s (on the left) exchange tonnage with Montana Western-leased Rarus GP9s at the old GN yard in Butte, June 19, 1987. (Left): Wedged between the abandoned Milwaukee Road roadbed and the Rarus (ex-BA&P) main line, a northbound Montana Western freight winds through Silver Bow Canyon on June 19, 1987, on rails that were once all alone here—and only three feet apart.

Epilogue—A Visit to Lombard

IT'S NOT EASY finding Lombard. Fishing access signs on the state highway at Toston don't help much, but maps do show a dirt road heading south to a spot where Sixteen Mile Creek flows into the Missouri River, allowing the Milwukee Road to loop over the Northern Pacific on a graceful curved bridge. A small railroad town once stood there too, but not anymore.

The trail to Lombard passes picnic tables set in the middle of a pasture, then climbs over a steep ridge where a fork in the road is marked, incongruously, by an ordinary street sign. It's all downhill from here.

The road twists down the mountainside, where glimpses of legendary Sixteen Mile Canyon and the abandoned Milwaukee Road line can be seen. Then, there it is: the Missouri River, BN's Helena main line skirting the east bank, and the trackless Milwaukee Road bridge that crosses them both.

It was the Montana Railroad that put Lombard on the map. Organized in 1893 to transport silver ore from the Castle Mountains to the NP main line at Lombard, Richard A. Harlow's Montana Midland Railroad completed only two miles of track before the Panic of 1893 brought about its demise. A reorganized Montana Railroad built east from Lombard across the Belt Mountains to Merino in 1900. The road's chief engineer, Arthur B. Lombard, renamed the latter town Harlowton after his boss, and in kind, Harlow named the junction town on the Missouri after Lombard. Milwaukee Road acquired the "Jawbone Line" (so named because of Harlow's ability to spread the blarney) for its transcontinental route in 1908.

At its zenith, Lombard was home to 800 people plus a hotel and school, and for a few days in 1916, hosted a circus (the nearby town of Ringling was named after the famous circus brothers). Both the Milwaukee Road and Northern Pacific maintained modest depots and an interchange yard, and from time to time, Milwaukee kept helpers for the 40-mile climb up Sixteen Mile Canyon.

The town of Lombard was abandoned in the late 1950s when the NP and Milwaukee agencies were closed and the interchange yard abandoned. The last Milwaukee Road train passed through town in 1980 and within a few years, its tracks were torn up, leaving only a gravel scar as a reminder of better times.

Even BN has forsaken Lombard; its siding here was removed in 1986 and the following year, the tracks themselves were leased to Montana Rail Link. There is some speculation that MRL may eventually abandon the Helena–Livingston–Billings line (BN's Helena–Great Falls–Billings line, though longer, would suffice). The "National Rail Defense Network" includes BN trackage from Great Falls to Helena and Garrison, but not the Helena–Billings line. Thus there is some possibility—however remote— that Lombard might someday lose the MRL as well.

★

The way out of Lombard is the same as the way in. At the top of the ridge, there's time for one last look. The loneliness felt in the wind seems appropriate, for Lombard has a way of reminding us of the frailty of man's enterprises, no matter how grand they might have been. Unlike other places that survived despite losses in rail service, there was nothing to sustain Lombard. It simply wasn't needed anymore.

So if or when MRL pulls out, this isolated part of the Northwest will be returned to nature. The impatient clatter of steel wheels will no longer compete with the eternal sounds of the Missouri River. And Lombard will fade further into obscurity.

Street sign on the ridge above Lombard. In the distance, Toston and the Missouri River Canyon.

Lombard, June 21, 1987: Nothing remains except a few old cars and a pile of railroad ties. NP's depot sat to the right of Milwaukee's Missouri River bridge, while the Milwaukee's was located where the dirt road curves away from the abandoned right-of-way. The NP–Milwaukee interchange track (the original 1893 Montana Railroad alignment) followed Sixteen Mile Creek from the NP depot, under the smaller Milwaukee bridge in the background, and up the canyon another half mile (see page 157).

Comings and goings in Lombard this June 21, 1987 morning included BN train No. 21, a Seattle-bound hotshot, swinging along the east bank of the Missouri River (below) and under the Milwaukee Road bridge (right).

(Opposite page): A last look at Sixteen Mile Canyon: No Little Joes, no *Olympian Hiawathas*. Just an empty roadbed, the mountains, and the wind.

Bibliography

BOOKS

Athearn, R.G.: *Union Pacific Country*. University of Nebraska Press, 1971.

Austin, E. and Dill, T.: *The Southern Pacific in Oregon*. Pacific Fast Mail, 1987.

Beebe, L.: *The Central Pacific and The Southern Pacific Railroads*. Howell North Books, 1963.

Bryan, E.A.: *Occident Meets Orient*. The Student Book Corporation, 1936.

Burrows, R.G.: *Railway Mileposts: British Columbia* (Volumes I and II). Railway Milepost Books, 1981/1984.

Colorado Rail Annual No. 15. Colorado Railroad Museum, 1981.

Culp, E.D.: *Stations West, the Story of the Oregon Railways.* Caxton Printers, 1972.

Derleth, A.: *The Milwaukee Road, Its First Hundred Years.* Creative Age Press, 1948.

Drury, G.H.: *The Train-Watcher's Guide to North American Railroads,* Kalmbach Publishing Co., 1984.

Drury, G.H.: *The Historical Guide to North American Railroads,* Kalmbach Publishing Co., 1985.

Dubin, A.D.: *Some Classic Trains.* Kalmbach Publishing Co., 1964.

Due, J.F. and Juras, F.: *Rails to the Ochoco Country.* Golden West Books, 1968.

Ehernberger, J.L. and Gschwind, F.G.: *Smoke Down the Canyons.* E&G Publications, 1966.

Ehernberger, J.L. and Gschwind, F.G.: *Smoke Along the Columbia.* E&G Publications, 1968.

Ferrell, M.H.: *Rails, Sagebrush and Pine.* Golden West Books, 1967.

Frey, R.L. and Schrenk, L.P.: *Northern Pacific Supersteam Era (1925–1945).* Golden West Books, 1985.

Green, R.: *The Northern Pacific Railway.* Northwest Shortline, 1985.

Hidy, R.W., Hidy, M.E., Scott, R.V. and Hofsommer, D.L.: *The Great Northern Railway.* Harvard Business School Press, 1988.

Hofsommer, D.L.: *The Southern Pacific, 1901–1985.* Texas A&M University Press, 1986.

Holbrook, S.H.: *The Age of Moguls,* Doubleday and Co., 1954.

Kratville, W.W.: *Motive Power of the Union Pacific,* Kratville Publications, 1960.

Lewis, E.A.: *American Shortline Railway Guide.* Kalmbach Publishing Co., 1986.

Lewty, P.J.: *To the Columbia Gateway.* Washington State University Press, 1987.

McArthur, A.: *Oregon Geographic Names,* Oregon Historical Society, 1974.

Middleton, W.D.: *When the Steam Railroads Electrified.* Kalmbach Publishing Co., 1974.

Nolan, E.W.: *Northern Pacific Views.* Montana Historical Society, 1983.

Olmsted, R.P.: *Milwaukee Rails.* McMillan Publications, 1980.

Pinkepank, J.A.: *The Second Diesel Spotters Guide.* Kalmbach Publishing Co., 1973.

Ranks, H.E. and Kratville, W.W.: *The Union Pacific Streamliners.* Kratville Publications, 1974.

Renz, L.T.: *The History of the Northern Pacific Railroad.* Ye Galleon Press, 1980.

Riegger, H.: *The Camas Prairie.* Pacific Fast Mail, 1986.

Sanford, B.: *McCulloch's Wonder.* Whitecap Books, 1981.

Sanford, B.: *Pictorial History of British Columbia.* Whitecap Books, 1981.

Scribbins, J.: *The Hiawatha Story.* Kalmbach Publishing Co., 1970.

Signor, J.R.: *Rails in the Shadow of Mt. Shasta.* Darwin Publications, 1982.

Steinheimer, R.: *The Electric Way Across the Mountains.* Carbarn Press, 1980.

Stindt, F.A.: *The Oregon Pacific and Eastern Railway.* Fred A. Stindt, 1983.

Strapac, J.A.: *Southern Pacific Motive Power Annual* (various issues, 1966–1973). Chatham Publishing Co., 1966–1974.

Wagner, F.H.: *Burlington Northern Motive Power Annual* (various issues, 1971–1983). Motive Power Services, 1971–1981.

Wagner, F.H.: *Union Pacific Motive Power Review 1968–1977.* Motive Power Services, 1978.

Wood, J.V.: *Railroads Through the Coeur d'Alenes.* Caxton Printers, 1983.

Woods, C.R.: *Lines West.* Superior Publishing Co., 1967.

Woods, C.R.: *The Northern Pacific.* Superior Publishing Co., 1968.

Woods, C.R.: *Milwaukee Road West.* Superior Publishing Co., 1972.

Woods, C.R. and D.M.: *Spokane, Portland and Seattle.* Superior Publishing Co., 1974.

Woods, C.R. and D.M.: *The Great Northern Railway.* Pacific Fast Mail, 1979.

Zimmerman, K.R.: *The Milwaukee Road Under Wire.* Quadrant Press, 1973.

Miscellaneous Publications

Business Week, McGraw-Hill Inc.

CTC Board, Hyrail Publications.

Inland Empire Rail Quarterly/Railway Review, Inland Empire Railway Historical Society.

Montana, the Magazine of Western History, Montana Historical Society, 1983.

Official Railway Guide (various editions), National Railway Publication Co.

Pacific News, Chatham Publishing Co.

Pacific Rail News, Interurban Press.

Passenger Train Journal, Interurban Press.

Rail Classics, Challenge Publications.

Railroad and Railfan, Carstens Publications.

Railroad Magazine.

Railway Quarterly, Challenge Publications.

Seattle Times.

Southern Pacific Bulletin, Southern Pacific Co.

The Dope Bucket, SP&S Rwy. Co.

The Milwaukee Electrification—A Proud Era Passes, Milwaukee Road Public Relations, 1973.

Trains Magazine, Kalmbach Publishing Co.

Index